MW00779350

Dear Reader,

About a year ago, Pranjal and I were discussing MarketsandMarkets' research on the $25 trillion transition happening in the global B2B economy, with new revenue streams replacing existing ones. Being the author that he is, Pranjal realized that this was the emergence of a new paradigm, Industry 5.0, and saw it as a perfect subject for his next breakthrough book. Over the next few months, Pranjal leveraged his engagement with the World Economic Forum (including the Davos meeting) to engage with business leaders to identify this new pattern.

Based on this $25 trillion shift, we concluded that tomorrow's winners would be those who envision and ideate about the future while driving business-case-oriented action to create value. We believed that our company's ecosystem, including our colleagues, customers, and well-wishers, was at the forefront of this progressive thinking. About 25% of the global economic shift will directly or indirectly impact 25% of the global population. If there is a way to help everyone monetize this shift rather than get adversely impacted by it by creating awareness ahead of time, we both thought there could not be a bigger and better purpose. So, we decided to create a guidebook for these leaders to navigate the uncertain future and emerge as winners, irrespective of the nature of disruption. MarketsandMarkets provided its research to Pranjal, and he continued his conversation with business leaders to write *The Next New*.

As you may have noticed, this book has already been recognized by business leaders across the world, such as Børge Brende, President of WEF and Former Minister of Foreign Affairs of Norway (2013–2017); Blake Moret, Chairman and Chief Executive Officer of Rockwell Automation, Inc.; Aiman Ezzat, CEO, Capgemini; Sabrina Soussan, Chairman and CEO, Suez; and Bracken P. Darrell, President and CEO, Logitech International.

There's a reason why such prominent business leaders are seeing this book as a global-scale event. We believe that the key to success in the future will not just be knowledge and skills, which machines can significantly substitute for, but rather a growth mindset and attitude. This book is a practical handbook for everyone wishing to develop this mindset, succeed in their career, and impact their business. *The Next New* offers practical strategies and insights for leaders to adapt and thrive in this fast-changing business landscape.

We hope you will enjoy reading *The Next New* and share it with your colleagues and teammates who you believe could benefit from developing a growth mindset.

Over the next few months, we will continue discussing ideas and actions for navigating the fifth industrial revolution with business leaders worldwide. We hope you will join us in this endeavor.

Thank you for your time and interest in the book.

Sandeep Sugla,
Founder & CEO,
MarketsandMarkets™ Research Pvt. Ltd.

# THE
# *NEXT*
# *NEW*

Dear Calvin
Hope you enjoy this
Chronicle of transformation

Prayag

MENLO PARK
JUNE 2023

Celebrating
30 Years of Publishing
in India

## Praise for *The Next New*

*The Next New* is a required—and compelling—reading for anyone looking to understand how the intersection of technological, societal and economic forces is ushering in a new era of opportunity not just for prosperity but for the well-being of our communities and planet.

**Børge Brende, president, World Economic Forum**

*The Next New* shows clearly that the rules of the game are changing around how value is created. And, hence, how businesses innovate, produce, operate and engage with their customers. However, as Pranjal Sharma explains, the fifth industrial revolution opens up opportunities for organizations to do business in new and better ways. Sustainable transformation is the challenge of our generation to ensure growth and opportunity for all. Pranjal's book is a testament to this.

**Aiman Ezzat, CEO, Capgemini**

In our technology-led and fast-changing world, we need more than ever to take a step back and analyse the developments taking place in our societies. By placing social and environmental issues at the core of the fifth industrial revolution that he describes, Pranjal Sharma not only proposes a new, ambitious approach, but invites us to follow the only path that can respond to the emergencies of our time.

**Sabrina Soussan, chairman and CEO, SUEZ**

This is a book that needed to be written. Pranjal nails it in his understanding of how sustainability and social impact are the cornerstone of all future technology breakthroughs.

**Bracken P. Darrell, president and CEO,
Logitech International**

# THE
# *NEXT*
# *NEW*

## *NAVIGATING THE FIFTH*
## *INDUSTRIAL REVOLUTION*

## PRANJAL SHARMA

**HARPER**
BUSINESS

*An Imprint of* HarperCollins *Publishers*

First published in India by Harper Business
An imprint of HarperCollins *Publishers* 2023
4th Floor, Tower A, Building No. 10, DLF Cyber City,
DLF Phase II, Gurugram, Haryana – 122002
www.harpercollins.co.in

2 4 6 8 10 9 7 5 3 1

P-ISBN: 978-93-5629-564-3
E-ISBN: 978-93-5629-565-0

Typeset in 11.5/15.2 Apollo MT Std at
Manipal Technologies Limited, Manipal

Printed and bound at
Replika Press Pvt. Ltd, India

MIX
Paper from
responsible sources
FSC® C016779

This book is produced from independently certified FSC® paper to ensure
responsible forest management.

*The ignorant work for their own profit, the wise work for the welfare of the world.*

—The Bhagavad Gita

# Contents

*Foreword by Blake Moret*                                   ix

*Prologue*                                                 xiii

*Introduction by Aashish Mehra*                           xxiii

1.  Flying New Frontiers                                      1

2.  Planting in Air, Earth and Water                        23

3.  The Chemistry of Chemicals                              43

4.  Smart Manufacturing Advances Further                    61

5.  Automotive for the People                               78

6.  Vectors of Changing Sectors                             97

7.  Firing Up Green Digital Energy                         116

8.  High-Tech Healthcare                                   134

9.  Weapons of Mass Disruption                             156

*Epilogue*                                                 173

*Notes and References*                                     179

*Index*                                                    197

*A Special Thank You*                                      213

*Acknowledgements*                                         215

# Foreword

In the last few years, perhaps no word was called upon more often than 'unprecedented' to describe the state of the world. It is our nature to look for extremes whatever time we are in, but there are plenty of reasons for the uniqueness of this period—the pandemic, supply chain shortages, workforce upheaval, climate change, inflation and red-hot geopolitical strife. But which of these are transitory and cyclical, and which ones are groundbreaking harbingers of brand-new technologies, processes, business models and even ethical systems? In *The Next New*, Pranjal Sharma surveys a broad landscape to provide insight into the true disrupters affecting all of us.

My industry—manufacturing—provides a front-row seat to the upheaval. As a result of the recent seismic pressures, it has experienced dramatically accelerated change—effectively twenty years of evolution in the short span of three years. Companies that were considering remote commissioning and operation of production lines had to quickly put plans into action, with travel and face-to-face contact limited during the pandemic. The need was urgent, as we saw the high degree of dependency on making products—from food to clean water to medicine and transportation—fast and with good quality. Skilled workers, energy and automation are needed to provide eight billion individuals of the world with even a basic standard of living.

Technology continues to play an enabling role, but people are still the stars. Process automation, robotic material handling, artificial intelligence (AI), digital twins and other technologies of the fourth industrial revolution have amazing capabilities, but engaged and enabled people are still required to plan, commission, operate and optimize the tools. When a people-centric approach is applied to technology implementation, we see improvement in nearly every aspect of the manufacturing operation, from efficiency, productivity and maintenance to energy use and worker safety. The digital transformation has placed manufacturing at the intersection of technology and society and requires a fundamental shift in the way an organization and its people think about their work and their processes. Culture change is at the heart of a successful digital transformation journey.

Pranjal captures this paradigm shift, arguing how the industry is experiencing the birth of the fifth industrial revolution—which he calls a more caring era—and the end of the fourth industrial revolution—which he concludes was driven by the goal to derive maximum cost and time efficiency, at times without considering the impact on society.

Since his last book, *India Automated: How the Fourth Industrial Revolution Is Transforming India*, Pranjal notes a global 'new improved version of a technology-based transformation' that factors in the impact of social inclusion, environmental sustainability and improved accountability. The *Rockwell Automation 2023 State of Smart Manufacturing Report* found 97 per cent of the participants reporting plans to use smart manufacturing technology to enable and optimize more agile and resilient production processes, empower the workforce, manage risk, drive sustainability and accelerate transformation.

Pranjal explores numerous examples of technology-based transformation, in industries as diverse as aerospace, agriculture and basic materials production. He links what is possible with how it should be implemented to provide the best outcomes. We all want the sources of the material things we need to be resilient, agile and sustainable. Resilient to cybersecurity attacks. Agile to produce more customized products with little or no changeover time. Sustainable to maximize efficient use of scarce resources. Pranjal's native country—India—is witnessing a spectacular pace of digitalization across all sectors, giving him a first-hand perspective on the power of this transformation.

Prepared people are core to the success of making things. The winning hand is a highly trained, engaged workforce working in concert with cutting-edge technology and automation. In this regard, Pranjal raises another critical point—companies leveraging advanced manufacturing technology must plan for not only the investment in innovative technologies, but also for the training and skills of their workforce. The world is facing a worker shortage, a problem across mature and developing economies alike. In manufacturing, digital technologies stretch scarce talent and keep workers safer. Such tools as augmented reality and machines equipped with artificial intelligence effectively give workers 'superpowers'. These advancements help create more efficient and agile processes, improve safety and shorten training time. Cloud-based solutions can help democratize the landscape, putting world-class technology within reach of small- and medium-sized businesses almost anywhere in the world. The technology also makes manufacturing jobs more inclusive and realistic for a wider-ability group by enabling machines to carry out heavy lifting and other physically challenging tasks. It keeps humans out of hazardous environments and reduces the risk of repetitive injuries and accidents.

Pranjal makes a compelling argument that people, and our planet, must take priority during the fifth industrial revolution. In manufacturing, we are working to ensure a future where humanity can thrive. Truly sustainable endeavors, powered by the technologies of the fifth industrial revolution, will expand human possibility.

**Blake Moret**
Chairman and CEO
Rockwell Automation, Inc.
Milwaukee, Wisconsin, USA

# Prologue

The fourth industrial revolution is a lived reality now. What seemed like an arcane phrase a few years ago has now percolated deep into the thoughts and actions of business leaders and policymakers. Now, the next phase has begun. The fifth industrial revolution is upon us. This may appear like a forced application of an existing phrase. This is a new improved version of a technology-based transformation.

The fourth industrial revolution was about the application of emerging technologies which were connected, interactive and intuitive. The end objective was to derive the maximum cost and time efficiency. The impact on society was not always a factor.

The fifth improves upon the fourth. It is more caring. The additional objectives are sustainability, governance and social impact. Technological solutions that factor in the impact of social inclusion, environmental sustainability and improved accountability form the fifth industrial revolution. This adds a layer of humanity to existing and emerging technologies.

The rise of technologies like artificial intelligence, process automation and unmanned vehicles should not be at a human cost. Nor should it be at the cost of the planet. Ensuring that humans work in a mutually beneficial manner while minimizing the impact on earth is a key feature of the new industrial revolution.

Business rules are being redefined by the ethics- and values-based demands of ESG or environment, social and governance norms.[1]

The objectives of achieving the sustainable development goals of the United Nations is inspiring global policies and investments in a range of socially important activities.[2]

The rising investment in digital public infrastructure is a symbol of the focus on creating business models that help the society and not only the shareholders. Emerging markets like India are leading the charge on creating digital public infrastructure. Issues of digital divide, financial inclusion, education and access to healthcare are being addressed using tech platforms at scale. Companies and governments are driven by a whole of society approach. 'The world needs a new playbook for digital infrastructure that mediates the flow of people, money and information. This will facilitate countries looking to digitally empower their citizens. They can then rapidly build platforms that address the specific needs of people, while ensuring people are able to trust and use the platform— without fear of exclusion or exploitation,' writes Samir Saran, president of Observer Research Foundation.[3]

If the fifth industrial revolution were to be represented as a mathematical equation, this is how it would be.

(ESG + Fourth industrial revolution) × SDGs
= Fifth industrial revolution

The 5IR can well be described as technology-led transformations which are guided by the values of ESG with sustainable development goals as an objective. A combination of such forces and shifts are leading to deep changes in consumer preferences, policy changes and the creative destruction of centuries old business models. *The Next New* is about the new phase of industrial revolution which will be determined by ESG values and SDGs objectives.

The three forces of technological breakthroughs, demand for social inclusion and need for sustainable development are causing global shifts in business models.

This book captures the impact of these three forces with examples and predictions for various sectors.

The key pillars of the fifth industrial revolution are:

- Technological breakthroughs: Rise of AI, material science, new fuels, among others
- Values, ethics, safety and social equity: Increased governance with focus on social inclusion
- Climate change goals and accountability: Tech will be expected to serve the objective of sustainability and accountability of actions

Sustainable technologies are not only about renewables and electric vehicles. It is also about using the new technologies for measuring and mitigating the impact of human action on the ecology. In this book, you will read about examples of the use of green hydrogen, green pesticides, sustainable manufacturing and lightweighting of materials to reduce energy consumption.[4]

This, thus, is the deep change we see around us. It is happening faster than we can comprehend sometimes. Capturing change has never been easy, especially when it is rapid and transformative. Today, business models are changing faster than the ability of CEOs to understand, absorb and adapt to them. Agility is not about changing in three years; it is about shifting policies and processes in three months.

Managing change has never been easy. And today change is on every front: technology, regulation, geopolitics, consumer preferences and climate concerns. Each is influencing and changing the other in unpredictable ways. This confluence of forces is bearing down on business models at a blistering pace and making the smartest of business leaders hesitate in forming confident predictions about the future.

Heroes are the ones who can predict a business environment within six months hence. A war, a pandemic, an AI chatbot that knows more than most of us, consumers who prefer to rent not acquire—it increasingly appears that success and failure are a game of chance and not skill anymore.

Astute business leaders must become more adept at this game. Chance has a role but it cannot overwhelm skill. It is important to take a longer view of business models and abandon current models and explore new ideas.

Now it has become easier to read a multitrillion-dollar transition of a business model than many would have imagined. It may appear overwhelming at first but once the various parts of the business have been broken down and the impact of the impending shifts understood, the new business model appears far more reasonable.

Confronted with change, CEOs often loathe giving up a revenue-generating model. They hold on to a dying structure and lament when it collapses. However, real leadership lies in being ahead of the change. The mettle is tested when businesses change before they are forced to. They mature when they give up current profit for long-term survival. They survive by abandoning the old and aggressively adopting the new. 'The world is evolving into a completely new economy. Call it the automation economy, because automation has to be the foundation of how we operate every aspect of our business. And when we do that, automation gives you agility. Agility is the foundation of stability in a world of uncertainty,' says Mihir Shukla, CEO and cofounder of US-based Automation Anywhere.[5]

The signs are starkly visible. The healthcare sector is huge. Today each of its segments is changing rapidly. Data is automatically flowing from every medical instrument. Medicines are being tested by an algorithm. A digital health twin will allow an expert to diagnose deeper and faster. The hospital of tomorrow will have to totally reorganize its existing process. From diagnostics to devices to data-flows, each aspect of the vast healthcare sector is transforming before our eyes.

We rely so much on search engines. These too could be disrupted. A debate has already been triggered about the possibility of increasingly sophisticated chatbots becoming the new search engines. This is entirely possible. Currently, most chatbots, including ChatGPT, source their information from a vast yet limited set of data. It is limited to information and developments till the end of 2021. Search engines are current and keep updating information. Chatbots are far more articulate in their response and bring more focus to a query that a search engine like Google finds difficult to manage. However,

ChatGPT's human-like response neither mentions the source of the information nor does it offer links or citations.

The synthesized and anonymized information is both useful and tricky as it will be difficult to confirm the veracity of the information in the chatbot. The ease of conversation with ChatGPT made waves across the world. The chatbot is being tested and trained with thousands of questions and chats being done by enthusiasts. Anyone can log in and chat with ChatGPT. Each conversation is research and feedback for the developers. We also have to be cautious. A chatbot doesn't know everything. While its expression and writing is like a human, its information may be incorrect and flawed. All users should crosscheck each information and not blindly accept everything that a chatbot says. Similar worries were expressed when Google and other search engines were launched. Even with them we have to be sure about the sources of information and facts.

There are several frontiers that chatbots have to cross. The data set that determines the response can keep increasing. It can also be domain-specific for different chatbots. So a healthcare chatbot can be only for patients while another can be used for students of mathematics. Digital interaction is moving from text to voice with options of many languages. To go beyond search engines and voice-based assistants like Alexa, chatbots will need greater amounts of information that can be accessed in various languages and voices. Chatbots are evolving rapidly and would have several new versions in ensuing months.

There is already a level of convergence between chatbots, search engines and digital assistants. While they complement each other, they are being integrated into easy-to-use solutions. Machine learning and voice recognition technologies are changing rapidly enough to indicate that many business models and functions are ripe for disruption. As chatbots are linked to a larger pool of information and connected to the internet, the multibillion-dollar search engine business model could collapse overnight. Microsoft's OpenAI has to compete with DeepMind, an AI company owned and supported by Google. DeepMind has achieved several major AI milestones spanning a range of disciplines since it was founded in 2010, including beating human world champions at the complex board game Go and predicting over 200 million structures of all known proteins. Sparrow chatbot claims to have better features than OpenAI's ChatGPT. According to some experts, Sparrow has the ability to cite sources through reinforcement learning. In a blog post, DeepMind has explained that Sparrow could be used to train other chatbots to be safer and more useful. 'Sparrow is a research model and proof of concept, designed with the goal of training dialogue agents to be more helpful, correct, and harmless. By learning these qualities in a general dialogue setting, Sparrow advances our understanding of how we can train agents to be safer and more useful—and ultimately, to help build safer and more useful artificial general intelligence (AGI),' the blog says. In many ways, this is the essence of the fifth industrial revolution. Ensuring that smart and breakthrough advances in technology are built with guardrails which prevent harm while maximizing benefits to industry and society.[6]

Customer care to personal assistants to search engines could soon evolve and explode with ever smarter chatbots that do more than just chatting.

In this context, let us examine the robotic automation process or RPA that helped bring transparency and efficiency to businesses. It has already evolved in the last few years to a totally new version. The next evolution of RPA is intelligent process automation or IPA. As per an assessment by Cognizant, 'RPA takes repetitive manual tasks and uses bots, or software robots, to replace them with automated workflows. IPA goes a step further, adding advanced cognitive technologies such as AI to expand business process automation across the entire enterprise.'

In short, while RPA is the automation of a process that repeats itself blindly, IPA adds its thinking cap. The IPA process mimics the way humans think and can resolve conflicts far better than a classic automation process. In some ways, IPA is constantly analysing the results of its efforts to improve the outcome. Intelligence technologies such as computer vision (converting scans to text) and natural language processing are part of the IPA. In the normal process of automation, if a customer enters data wrongly or in an incorrect box, the process will not work. But the artificial intelligence inherent in IPA will allow it to assess the information even if it is not structured.

When a customer sends queries to a chatbot, a few standardized answers pop up. If the questions from a customer are specific to a region or a product, the chatbot is unable to answer. However, an IPA-based chatbot will go beyond the standard answers to search for relevant information from its database and then respond to a customer.

RPA companies are working with their clients to add intelligence to their tools. Robots extend the scope of automation to knowledge-based processes that otherwise could not be covered. When companies assess their social media reputation or customer-satisfaction levels, the automation tool must understand the context. Here, intelligent analysis of comments, feedback or social posts requires IPA.

Tech companies are enabling a high level of efficiency with IPA tools for their clients. Cognizant says it helped a credit card service company achieve 99 per cent accuracy in handling 1,00,000 vendor invoices each month. And for a leading agribusiness company, IPA led to a 90 per cent process improvement and a 400 per cent improvement in return on investment. 'IPA mimics activities carried out by humans and, over time, learns to do them even better. Traditional levers of rule-based automation are augmented with decision-making capabilities thanks to advances in deep learning and cognitive technology,' says a McKinsey report. 'The promise of IPA is radically enhanced efficiency, increased worker performance, reduction of operational risks and improved response times and customer journey experiences.'[7]

Shukla says, 'Automation is the next chapter in the technology evolution, with a brand-new set of technologies.' He adds that this will also allow companies to grow their businesses and connect with customers in a way never done before.

'This is a necessary transformation for all businesses. We are going to operate in a world that will require speed, scale, agility and ability to operate more efficiently. And automation is a key part of that solution.'

Companies in nearly every sector can use the new generation of process automation. The ability of IPA to create efficiency is impacting manufacturing and services. Within enterprises and even government agencies, the use of IPA can be useful. From invoice processing to revenue-cycle management, companies can reduce their cost of finance. Healthcare claims and payroll management can be enhanced for government agencies that are often the largest employers in the world. Once a competitive advantage, IPA is nearly a necessity now.

Such is the nature of change. Just when we think that a new model has matured and has dominated a market segment, along comes a new idea that washes the old one away. The transitions mentioned in this book are but a few of the thousands that are occurring even as you read. Business leaders and policymakers must prepare for these transitions. The changes captured in this book are a precursor. While this book looks at the scenarios in the next few years, the changes could happen in months. The research done by MarketsandMarkets has been able to quantify the impact of disruptions across sectors. Within each sector there are multiple sub-sectors and niche business. Each is highly valuable and global in its impact. MarketsandMarkets Research was ranked among the best management consulting firm in the US by Forbes magazine in March 2023. It is the only startup from India to be in the list.[8]

Welcome to the Fifth Industrial Revolution where technologies are being driven to serve the needs of society, humanity and ecology. And in the process triggering a multitrillion-dollar business disruption.

# Introduction

## *The Global Transition*

'May you live in interesting times.'

—A Chinese proverb

Perhaps this proverb best sums up the changes we are likely to witness in the coming decade. The pace of disruption around us is increasing, and new ecosystems and industries are being created at an unprecedented pace. A decade back, how many experts would have placed bets on a significant shift to remote working, telemedicine/remote patient monitoring challenging mainstream healthcare delivery, hydrogen-powered mobility, or gene therapy as a cure for cancer? But we are seeing these changes take shape, and that too at a dramatic pace.

There has also been a growth in the interconnectedness between industries and ecosystems, with disruptions in one ecosystem impacting many others. At MarketsandMarkets, we research a host of megatrends such as artificial intelligence (AI), connectivity and blockchain, and the disruption they are causing across multiple end-use industries, which, in turn, is leading to the creation of new revenue and growth opportunities. For instance, 'sustainability' as a megatrend is disrupting multiple ecosystems—it is leading to decarbonization in power and utilities, and heavy industries such as steel and cement. This consecutively is creating new revenue sources for companies across ecosystems—green hydrogen, green ammonia, carbon capture utilization and storage (CCUS), fuel cells, energy storage and smart grids in the energy industry; electric vehicles (EVs), electric aircraft, electric ships in the transportation industry; recycled plastics, recyclable lithium-ion batteries, biodegradable polymers in the chemicals industry and an opportunity for technology companies to offer digital twin for real-time asset management, green data centres and AI-based energy management solutions.

These are just a few examples of the disruptions being caused across multiple interconnected ecosystems. The ensuing schematic diagram and table offer a few more examples.

## Megatrends + Industry = Disruptions → Opportunities

| Megatrend/ Shift | Industry | Disruption | Top Opportunities |
|---|---|---|---|
| COVID-19 | Cloud/IT | Remote work | Unified communication and collaboration: US$68 billion Edge computing: US$37 billion Virtual event platform: US$10 billion |
| Energy crisis | Automotive, aviation, marine | Electrification | Electric vehicle: four million units Electric aircraft: US$8 billion Electric ships: US$4.6 billion |
| Sustainability | Power | Clean energy | Hydrogen generation: US$142 billion Distributed energy resource management: US$0.3 billion Fuel cells: US$0.33 billion |
| COVID-19 | Healthcare | Remote patient monitoring | Telehealth: US$39 billion Wearable healthcare devices: US$18 billion |

| Megatrend/ Shift | Industry | Disruption | Top Opportunities |
|---|---|---|---|
| Sustainability | Food and beverage | Plant-based/ cultured alternatives | Plant-based meat: US$4.3 billion Cultured meat |
| Technological advancements (Blockchain) | Financial services | Cryptocurrency | Cryptocurrency: US$1.6 billion Crypto asset management: US$0.5 billion |
| Technological advancements (Automation) | Manufacturing | Robotics, internet of things (IoT) | Industrial robotics: US$42 billion Industrial IoT: US$77 billion |

## The US$25 Trillion Shift

At MarketsandMarkets, we expect that a staggering US$25 trillion worth of new markets or revenue sources will evolve in the coming decade. In this book, we will explore in detail the emerging technologies and markets contributing to this US$25 trillion worth of new revenue sources.

## Energy Sector

Sustainability, energy storage, digital technologies, and smart transmission and distribution are four megatrends that are shaping the future of power and utilities globally. We will discuss them here in this chapter.

## Sustainability

Sustainability alone as a megatrend is likely to create new revenue opportunities worth US$4.7 trillion across numerous end-use industries in the decade ahead.

## AEROSPACE & DEFENSE
- Electric Aircraft - $9
- Smart Airports - $7
- Electric Ship - $5
- Sustainable Aviation Fuel - $2

## HEALTHCARE
- Wearable Healthcare Devices - $30
- Environmental Monitoring - $18
- Medical Waste Management - $9
- Air Quality Monitoring System - $5

## FOOD & BEVERAGE, AGRICULTURE
- Eco-friendly Food Packaging - $80
- Protein Ingredients - $ 75
- Commercial Greenhouse - $56
- Plant Extracts - $55
- Plant-Based Beverages - $27
- Agricultural Biologicals - $21
- Essential Oils - $16
- Plant-based Protein - $15
- Agricultural Microbials - $13
- Organic Feed - $10
- Biopesticides - $9
- Plant-Based Meat - $9

## INFORMATION & COMMUNICATIONS TECHNOLOGY
- Smart Cities - $873
- IoT in Smart Cities - $312
- Smart City Platforms - $258
- Smart Transportation - $173
- Smart Buildings - $121
- Smart Learning - $95
- Internet of Things (IoT) in Utilities - $69
- Green Data Centre - $59
- Digital Logistics - $56
- Green Technology and Sustainability - $46
- Smart Water Management - $22

## AUTOMOTIVE & TRANSPORTATION
- Exhaust Heat Recovery System - $71
- Green Tires - $69
- EV Battery - $57
- E-bike - $33
- Battery Recycling - $23
- Lithium-Ion Battery Recycling - $14

## ENERGY & POWER
- Environmental Technology - $690
- Waste Management - $542
- Smart Grid - $103
- Hydrogen Generation - $78
- Offshore Wind - $56
- Blockchain in Energy - $38
- Offshore Wind - $25
- Concentrating Solar Power - $8
- Solid Oxide Fuel Cell - $4
- Residential Energy Management - $4

## CHEMICALS & MATERIALS, PACKAGING, CONSTRUCTION, MINING & MINERALS
- Sustainable Plastic Packaging - $123
- Bioethanol - $73
- Wastewater Treatment Services - $71
- Water Treatment Chemicals - $61
- Recycled Plastics - $43
- Plastic Waste Management - $40
- Point-of-Use Water Treatment Systems - $25
- Battery Recycling - $24
- Post-Consumer Recycled Plastics - $19
- Industrial Wastewater Treatment Chemicals - $16
- Precious Metals E-Waste Recovery - $12

## SEMICONDUCTOR & ELECTRONICS
- Smart Factory - $135
- Photovoltaic - $122
- Smart Manufacturing - $110
- Smart Appliances - $76
- Industrial Control & Factory Automation - $64
- Smart Home - $54
- Smart Lighting - $27
- Solar Lighting System - $14
- Smart Greenhouse Market - $2

Source: MarketsandMarkets MI Cloud
Note: Figures in US$, billions

US$4.7 trillion worth of revenue opportunities from sustainability

The wider energy transition has opened up a host of new revenue opportunities such as green hydrogen economy, carbon capture and utilization, new renewable energy sources, including offshore wind or quantum dots, energy and battery storage, bio-based fuels, smart transmission and distribution assets (smart grids and microgrids) and digital technologies (for instance, AI and blockchain).

Green hydrogen is among the cleanest fuels available in the market, and it is offering tremendous opportunities to decarbonize the existing energy system. Numerous factors are likely to drive its growth—a 40 per cent to 80 per cent reduction in the cost of production, favourable fiscal policies by the European Union governments, higher efficiencies in production due to technological advancements in electrolysis technologies and a strong demand from hydrogen-powered EVs and marine transportation.

CCUS is also a significant step towards achieving net-zero emission goals. Many factors are likely to have a significant role in the growth of CCUS—government incentives including tax credits, rising demand for $CO_2$ in processes including Enhanced Oil Recovery (EOR) in upstream oil and gas and in natural gas processing, and improvements in carbon capture technologies are some of them.

## Energy Storage

Energy storage is gaining prominence in reducing peak demand charges. It is also helping in integrating renewable sources, regulating voltage and frequency, and providing a backup power supply. The energy storage market is expected to be US\$15 billion by 2026 as advancements are anticipated in technologies such as lithium-ion batteries, flow batteries, sodium-based batteries, nickel-cadmium batteries, nickel-metal hydride, nickel-iron batteries and flywheel batteries.

## Leveraging Digital Technologies

The AI, IoT and blockchain are reshaping the energy industry. The IoT in the energy market is expected to be US$35 billion by 2026. It aims to enhance operational effectiveness, provide analytics-based decisions, improve production and offer upgraded security and proper management of assets. Blockchain in energy is expected to be a US$68 billion market. It is making electricity a tradeable asset by enabling commerce such as variable electricity rates, energy payments and peer-to-peer energy trading while offering low transaction costs and network transparency. AI is being leveraged to forecast energy demand and predict equipment breakdown and outages. This will result in smarter asset management, higher efficiencies and reduction in wastage.

## Smart Transmission and Distribution

Technological advancements have reshaped and transformed the electrical grid infrastructure as well. Electrical grids are becoming smarter as a result of the integration of IoT, cloud, analytics and smart devices from generation to transmission and distribution. The smart grid market is expected to be US$103 billion by 2026. Factors such as upgradation and modernization of the aging transmission and distribution infrastructure, restriction in electricity theft and interconnection of the existing grids with new ones are driving the smart grid market.

The microgrid market is also estimated to be US$42.3 billion by 2026. The market is growing as a result of the rising focus on decarbonization by various end users, government incentives, increasing demand for uninterrupted power supply, growing adoption of microgrids for rural electrification and rising instances of cyber-attacks on energy infrastructures.

## Chemicals and Materials Sector

The chemistry and advanced materials sector will be a key enabler of a fourth industrial revolution. Electric vehicles, drones, smartphones, high-speed internet and many other sectoral innovations require massive support from the chemicals and materials sector. Examples include using chlorosilanes in cables to deliver fiberoptic properties needed for fast and trouble-free data transfer; plastics, composites and batteries in EVs and drones; and substrates, backplanes and transparent conductors for smartphones and tablets.

Sustainability is a key theme impacting the chemical industry, and green chemicals, biodegradable/recyclable plastics, EV fluids and sustainable bio-lubricants have become focus areas for most players. Several startups are working on different solutions that promise bio-based and sustainable chemicals. From bioplastics and plant-based surfactants used for manufacturing detergents to natural fibres and environment-friendly materials, startups are working on a series of bio-based alternatives. The French startup Evertree is developing sustainable alternatives to fossil fuel-based industrial chemicals. It produces adhesive solutions that are bio-sourced instead of being petro-sourced resins. Its Green Ultimate product uses 60 per cent less fossil carbon to manufacture than a urea-formaldehyde resin.

Plastics, especially single-use plastics, have become the most significant environmental pollutant. Most countries have started implementing strict regulations regarding their usage. Many chemical companies are working hard to replace conventional plastics with compostable, biodegradable, oxo-degradable and bio-based plastics. Consequently, the global biodegradable plastics market is set to grow from US$7.7 billion in 2021 to US$23.3 billion by 2026, at a compound annual growth rate (CAGR) of 24.9 per cent.

Similarly, there is increasing adoption of sustainable adhesives and sealants. Sustainable adhesives belong to one of the three groups: solventless adhesives, waterborne adhesives and bio-based adhesives. New forms of renewable adhesives include adhesives made from beeswax and plants, recyclable adhesives, biodegradable and compostable green adhesives and repulpable adhesives.

In the materials industry, one of the most important trends is lightweighting. Natural fibre composites are disrupting the lightweighting material market and emerging as alternatives to glass fibre composites in many end-use industries such as automotive parts, building structures and consumer goods. In the new aircraft programmes of Boeing and Airbus, such as the 787 Dreamliner, 777X and A350XWB group, composites comprise 50 per cent of all materials used. According to MarketsandMarkets estimates, the global lightweighting material market size was estimated to be US$90 billion in 2021 and is expected to reach US$130 billion by 2026 at a CAGR of 7.6 per cent over 2021–26.

Another important trend impacting the materials industry is 3D-printed materials. High-performance plastic has emerged as a key material in the 3D-printing material market. 3D printing with high-performance plastics is useful in producing complex and intricate parts as it can withstand extreme temperature conditions. Aircraft and auto manufacturers are considering this quality to integrate high-performance thermoplastics into their manufacturing. Bioceramics such as hydroxyapatite and tricalcium phosphate have also disrupted the medical and healthcare 3D-printing market. These and other trends will be explored in detail in the chapter on chemicals and materials.

## Food and Agriculture Sector

Five trends will be disrupting the food and agriculture sector in the next ten years: smart or digital farming techniques, agrigenomics, new frontiers in farming, plant-based alternatives and food tech.

## Smart or Digital Farming

Agriculture is transforming into a technologically intense and data-driven industry as more companies embrace technologies such as AI, blockchain, IoT and remote sensing in agriculture. Blockchain is creating an efficient supply chain that allows one to trace products and improve transactional efficiencies. The IoT technologies are being leveraged for precision farming to collect farm-related data to boost the productivity of farmlands, and use farm robots, autonomous farm vehicles and agricultural drones with sensors for imaging, mapping and surveying of fields. The AI is being leveraged to process weather, soil, moisture and temperature data to help farmers in better sowing or harvesting decisions. Image processing, when combined with AI, is helping farmers monitor the health of the crops. It is also guiding agricultural robots in the targeted application of pesticides.

## New Frontiers in Agriculture

The next frontier in farming includes advanced and improved methods such as vertical farming and other indoor systems for growing hydroponic, aeroponic and aquaponics crops in an artificial environment created inside a facility using technology. It can help grow plants with high nutritious content in a shorter period as compared to traditional farming. This is critical given the twin challenges of increasing food demand and reducing arable land globally.

## Agrigenomics

The global agrigenomics market is majorly fuelled by rapid advances in the functional genomics sector with the massive adaptation of parallel sequencing technologies and the development of protocols to efficiently analyse cellular behaviour at the molecular level. We are seeing the adoption of molecular marker-assisted crop breeding leading to increased scope, speed and efficiency of crop selection. Advanced genome characterization techniques have shown increased quality and yield of crops. At the same time, they require less fertilizers, pesticides and water. For livestock, novel technologies are known to have greatly improvised desirable traits, such as milk yield, meat quality and reproductive life. Beyond food and nutritional security, tools and techniques of genome analysis can assist in detecting food safety issues such as spoilage and contamination, adulteration and economic fraud and traceability over the entire supply chain from farm to fork.

## Plant-Based Alternatives to Meat and Dairy

Historically, meat has been the main source of protein in developed markets. However, a change in consumer preference and interest in plant-based protein sources due to their nutritional profile, inclination towards clean eating, rise in health concerns (such as lactose intolerance), environmental concerns and animal welfare have contributed to the growth of the plant-based protein sector.

Plant-based meat products are significantly replacing conventionally processed meat products, such as burgers, sausages and nuggets. These alternatives contain lower levels of saturated fat, cholesterol and calories than animal-based meat. They often contain higher levels of micronutrients, such as zinc, iron and calcium.

## Food Tech

The 3D-printed food, robotic kitchens, AI-driven flavours, blockchain in supply chains and automated warehouses are some of the technology-enabled disruptions in the food and beverages sector. The 3D-printed food offers the promise of reduced wastage and the creation of customized and precise dishes for the consumer. Robotic kitchens use a combination of sensors and optical cameras to map ingredients, cookware and utensils within the kitchen and prepare a meal precisely as per instructions. AI is leveraged to blend food, flavours and aromas to bring new and creative dishes. Blockchain is poised to greatly improve the performance of supply chains, especially the new permissioned blockchains where participation is restricted to known supply chain partners, data standards and governance rules. In addition to these, key factors such as maintaining quality, regulatory restrictions, seasonal changes, hygiene standards, low shelf life and higher scale of production are getting streamlined with digitization.

## Healthcare

Technology in the healthcare sector is a boon and is already revolutionizing the doctor—patient relationship. The shift to digitalization has resulted in copious amounts of complex data generated by hospitals and medical institutions, which can be used to increase the level of care for patients. Five major trends that are shaping healthcare include the AI in diagnostic imaging, using CRISPR for gene editing, advanced therapies and regenerative medicine and connected, digital labs.

## Diagnostic Imaging and Teleradiology

Advancements in diagnostic imaging, such as AI and big data, have resulted in improved and affordable patient care. Big data comprises analysing information generated from clickstream and web and social media interactions; readings from medical devices, such as sensors, electrocardiogram (ECG), X-ray, healthcare claims, billing records and biometric data. The AI, on the other hand, increases the efficiency of diagnostics. Big data and analytical solutions have grown exponentially in sophistication and adoption in the last decade and made healthcare one of the top five big data industries, especially in the US.

Teleradiology is enabling the transmission of diagnostic medical images from one location to another, where radiologists and physicians can access them. This is essential because few radiologist subspecialties are typically located in metropolitan cities. A breakthrough expected in the teleradiology domain is the advent of 3D report viewing, as the deployment and utilization of sophisticated computed tomography (CT) and magnetic resonance imaging (MRI) 3D imaging services increase data complexity.

## Genomics, NGS and Gene Editing

Genomics has several application areas, including identifying human genetic disorders, drug discovery, agriculture, veterinary sciences and forensics. The application of genomics in forensic studies has increased significantly with the advent of next-generation sequencing (NGS), mainly due to the products offered by Illumina, USA, designed explicitly for forensic science. Advancements in NGS technologies are further transforming the landscape through reduced sequencing platforms and systems costs, and the sequencing process itself. As precise diagnosis and personalized medicine can increase survival rates and reduce the financial burden on national health insurance programmes, governments across the globe are making significant investments in genome sciences.

CRISPR is one of the most powerful tools that has emerged as thin gene editing technology. Scientists are hopeful of not just treating but also cutting off the genes responsible for therapeutic indications, such as oncology and neurodegenerative diseases. CRISPR-Cas9 is a revolutionary genome-editing technique that facilitates the efficient and directed alterations of the eukaryotic genome. It also enables the introduction of insertion or deletion mutations, the deletion of large genomic loci and the introduction of specific small DNA changes.

Integration of AI in genomics is enabling faster and more efficient applications in precision medicine. Autoimmune diseases, infectious diseases and cancer have become increasingly difficult to treat using conventional methods that do not consider individual genetic, environmental and lifestyle differences. While AI implementation in medical care and management is still in its initial stages, it is showcasing high potential by seamlessly integrating large-scale patient data. AI-inspired machine learning methods leverage the volume and exponential growth of genomic data to translate genetic information into new unforeseen insights for safer, more effective and cost-efficient personalized healthcare.

## Advanced Therapy Medicinal Products

Advanced therapy medicinal products (ATMPs) are medicines and therapeutic treatments that include gene therapy medicinal products, somatic cell therapy medicinal products and tissue-engineered products. They offer cutting-edge innovation and hope to people suffering from diseases with limited or no therapeutic options. Regenerative medicine refers to methods of replacing or regenerating human cells, tissues or organs to restore or establish normal function. This includes cell therapies, tissue engineering, gene therapy and biomedical engineering techniques, as well as traditional treatments involving pharmaceuticals, biologics and devices. At present, owing to the high level of personalization required during the development of autologous therapies, the cost involved in delivering ATMPs to patients is extremely high. When there will be a reduction in the cost of these therapies and an increase in the insurance coverage, it will likely pave the future of treatment for ailments that cannot be cured using traditional methods.

## Future of Laboratories

The laboratories of the future envisage more digitized, automated and integrated workflow approaches compared to siloed methodologies currently being followed worldwide. The laboratories of the future will utilize cutting-edge transformative technologies to drive advancements in laboratory workflow that impacts the current landscape and the future evolution in terms of how they operate and perform. This could involve using virtual and sophisticated digital tools and advanced hardware that can promote the globalization of lab environments in an open, standardized and collaborative manner.

## Aerospace and Defence

Emerging technology in the aerospace and defence industry is helping leverage space for various terrestrial uses. It is also enabling scientists, researchers and entrepreneurs reduce project time and cost. Two critical shifts propelling the space industry are the miniaturization of satellites and use of artificial intelligence to understand the universe's dynamics.

In general, space exploration technologies are expected to undergo much more advancement in the next few decades than they had in the past. The industry has systematically reshaped itself with fundamental digital tools such as robotics, additive manufacturing/3D printing, augmented reality (AR) and Big data analytics. AI and blockchain are strengthening security and management solutions using data generated by space businesses. The industry is also embracing advancements such as integrated computer vision, voice recognition technology, advanced AR and high-performance space suits.

## Sustainable Aviation

With its commitment to net-zero emission goals, the aerospace and defence industry is relying heavily on technological innovations and digitization to reduce its emission levels. The use of sustainable fuels (SAF), electrification of aircraft and hydrogen-powered aircraft and the deployment of efficient aircraft on short routes are the four major ways by which the aviation industry is moving towards sustainability. Companies such as Airbus, Ampaire, MagniX and Eviation are flight-testing electric aircraft meant for private, corporate or commuter trips.

Urban air mobility is focusing on developing an alternative hydrogen-based aviation fuel that could be the key to sustainable air travel and contribute immensely to the industry's emissions-reduction strategy. Recent technological advancements in propulsion systems, fuel cells, fuel efficiency, cryogenic storage, hydrogen fuel extraction and aircraft structural design—specifically for hydrogen-powered aircraft—have driven the market for hydrogen-powered aircraft and taken the industry one step closer to meeting its sustainability goals.

## Advanced Military Capabilities

The demand for electronic warfare systems is expected to be driven by three main aspects: rapid technological advancements, rising focus on directed energy weapons and increasing need for electronic protection prowess in armed forces worldwide.

Electric short take-off and landing aircraft (eSTOLs) utilize battery technology and attain propulsive power from electricity. They are designed to reduce noise emissions in comparison to traditional helicopters and have an inbuilt compact turbine-powered generator to recharge batteries mid-flight. Another major technological breakthrough in the segment is the automatic air-to-air refuelling between an aerial tanker and a fighter aircraft. Technologies used in automatic refuelling include image processing, visual tracking algorithms, drones and new video-based ones.

## Digital Battlefields

The global digital battlefield market consists of components, technologies, platforms and applications. AI and the IoT have emerged as complementary technologies that are finding significant application in digital battlefield products for military exercises and critical missions. The data produced from digital battlefield devices and related sensors would be heterogeneous and require AI for analysis. When merged with the IoT, AI systems would be especially useful in regulating digital battlefield products, including military devices. The AI systems will do this by analysing transmitted data and controlling their operations to match user requirements. In a nutshell, aerospace and defence are at a juncture where they are navigating their organizations into the future, combating disruption and embracing a future powered by digitization.

## Advanced and Smart Manufacturing

Advanced and smart manufacturing refers to the use of advanced technologies such as IoT, AI and data analytics to optimize the production process and improve efficiency, quality and responsiveness. In the future, smart manufacturing is expected to continue to evolve and transform the manufacturing industry. IoT and AI in manufacturing are resulting in reduced manufacturing time, improved predictive maintenance, enhanced visibility of the supply chain and the possibility of remote repairs. MarketsandMarkets estimates the smart manufacturing market to register a CAGR of 18.5 per cent over 2022–27.

In addition to IoT and AI, a few other technologies are at the heart of advanced and smart manufacturing—advancements in wireless charging, digital twins, usage of drones and automated guided vehicles in factories, the use of collaborative robots and advancements in AI chipsets.

## Future of Wireless Charging

According to MarketsandMarkets, Industry 4.0 is expected to boost the adoption of wireless charging in various end-user segments. Automatic wireless charging technology will be used for mobile robots, drones and cordless tools and instruments.

This will eliminate the complex docking mechanism process, and labour-intensive manual recharging and battery replacement.

Radiofrequency (RF) charging transfers power to devices wirelessly. With over-the-air charging mechanisms, devices requiring charging must remain fixed in one place; this will ensure that they have a clear line of sight to the transmitter. Many companies are developing various solutions that can work over a distance of several feet. Cota, a wireless power-transfer technology, utilizes RF to send data and power over distances of more than fifteen feet. If equipped with near-field communication (NFC), wireless charging can be incorporated into computer accessories such as the touch pen, type cover and mouse. For instance, a touch pen incorporated with NFC technology can be charged if pressed against a tablet, or a mouse can be charged if placed on a conference table with charging pads. This approach is intuitive, efficient, convenient, flexible and hassle-free. Over-the-air wireless charging will be able to support a broad range of devices, including small, low-power devices such as hearing aids, fitness bands, sensors and similar devices.

## Digital Twin

Digital twin technology creates virtual models of a physical asset, process or system. It uses data obtained from sensors and algorithms to make reasonable projections about future processes, which can reduce operating costs and help extend the life of equipment and assets. NASA was an early adopter of this technology in the aerospace and defence industry. It used digital twin to monitor and control the space stations and spacecraft, and to ensure crew safety.[1]

With the growing adoption of the IoT, the concept of digital twinning is becoming prominent. Product design and development, machine and equipment health monitoring, predictive maintenance and dynamic optimization are the four largest application areas of digital twin.

## Use of Drones and AGVs in Factories

Drones are rapidly replacing applications of legacy services in the commercial sector as they can be remotely managed by human operators or even autonomously by onboard computers. Applications such as aerial surveys, filmography and search and rescue have become popular and mainstream due to the increasing proliferation of drones. Drones can accelerate internal delivery processes between production points and enhance storage in factories with less space. Autonomous drones are being tested to transport components within the production line. A pioneering project between SEAT SA and the Eurecat Centre explores the possibility of using drones to optimize logistics.

In addition to drones, smart factories are witnessing increasing adoption of automated guided vehicles (AGVs). These are programmed by software to identify positioning, movement and location. Implementation of AGVs enables just-in-time (JIT) delivery of raw material, computerized control of received assembled parts and tracking of shipped articles. AGVs were initially used as towing trailers to speed up production. Vehicle-to-everything (V2X) is the next big step that can unlock the power of AGVs and driverless cars. V2X includes enhanced augmented reality, cooperative driving, extended electronic (NLOS) vision and more precise positioning. It is expected to be a game changer for the industry.

## Collaborative Robots

Smart manufacturing is toggling between Industry 4.0 and Industry 5.0. The latter is largely defined by the new branch of industrial robotics called cobots or collaborative robots. By definition, a cobot is a robot that physically communicates with people in any shared workspace. Cobots are easy to set up and program, and can work alongside people by keeping a safe distance from humans. They can be tasked with laborious and monotonous work and thus let humans focus on work that requires knowledge and skill. According to MarketsandMarkets, the collaborative-robots segment is projected to grow at a CAGR of 43.4 per cent from 2021 to 2027.

## AI Chipsets

With AI deepening its strong foothold on the industrial spectrum, AI chipsets are set to emerge as the key solution for large-scale data processing. The AI chipsets, also known as AI accelerators, are specialized computer chips that enable high speeds and efficiencies required for large-scale AI-specific calculations. Edge AI chips, one of the most prominent trends in chip technology, can help run AI processing 'on the edge', that is, on devices that are not connected to the cloud. As per MarketsandMarkets, the global AI chipsets market is expected to grow at a CAGR of 40.1 per cent by 2026.

## Automotive Sector

The future of mobility is expected to see significant changes with the integration of new technologies and trends such as EVs, autonomous vehicles, shared mobility, and connectivity. These advancements are aimed at reducing carbon emissions, improving road safety, and making transportation more accessible and convenient. Additionally, the development of smart cities and infrastructure is likely to play a key role in shaping the future of mobility.

The global mobility ecosystem is evolving rapidly, and with it, the traditional business models for designing, manufacturing, selling, servicing and financing vehicles are changing. The automotive industry is shifting from a hardware-focused industry to a more software-driven one. Key features of this transition include the use of EVs, connected cars, mobility fleet sharing, car-as-a-service (CaaS) or mobility-as-a-service (MaaS), and onboard sensors.

## Autonomous Vehicles

Autonomous vehicles (AVs) have the potential to improve road safety, reduce traffic congestion, and offer convenient and accessible transportation options. However, the widespread adoption of AVs will require significant technological advancements and the resolution of various challenges such as cybersecurity, liability and regulatory issues. In addition, consumer trust and acceptance will also be critical factors that will determine the pace of adoption. Original equipment manufacturers in China, Japan and South Korea offer several car models with level-1 and level-2 semiautonomous features. The next frontier is level-4 and level-5 self-driving cars, which do not require a driver to be present in the vehicle. Leading companies such as Tesla, Waymo, General Motors, Nissan and Volvo are heavily investing in the development of these self-driving cars.

## Connected Vehicles

The future of connected cars is expected to be characterized by the widespread adoption of IoT and 5G technologies. Connected cars will have the ability to communicate with other vehicles, infrastructure, and the cloud, offering enhanced safety features, improved navigation and a more personalized driving experience.

The race to launch a fully autonomous car is gaining momentum. However, industry leaders must master connectivity protocols before launching autonomous vehicles to deliver V2X capabilities. A V2X comprises several components, including vehicle-to-vehicle (V2V), vehicle-to-infrastructure (V2I), vehicle-to-pedestrian (V2P) and vehicle-to-cloud (V2C) communications. In this multifaceted ecosystem, cars will talk to other cars, to infrastructure such as traffic lights or parking spaces, to smartphone-toting pedestrians and to data centres via cellular networks. V2P communication involves the detection of pedestrians on or near the roads. V2P detection systems can be implemented in vehicles to provide warnings to drivers. V2I connectivity is the wireless exchange of critical operational data between vehicles and the infrastructure. It is intended to mitigate vehicle crashes and enable a wide range of other safety, mobility and environmental benefits. V2V communication is the wireless exchange of data among vehicles traveling in the same vicinity, which offers opportunities for significant safety improvements. Emergency brake light warning, forward collision warning, intersection movement assist, blind spot and lane-change warning, do-not-pass warning and control loss warning are common V2V communication functions.

Connected vehicles will also bring new challenges such as cybersecurity risks, data privacy, and the need for standardization—which we need to overcome.

## Shared Mobility

The future of shared mobility is expected to be shaped by the integration of new technologies, changing consumer preferences, and the need for sustainable and accessible transportation options. The trend towards shared mobility, which includes ride-hailing services, car-sharing, bike-sharing, and other forms of shared transportation, is aimed at reducing the number of personal vehicles on the road, reducing emissions, and improving urban mobility.

In the coming years, we can expect to see the continued growth of shared mobility, as well as the introduction of new and improved services that offer increased convenience and accessibility. The integration of autonomous technologies, electrification and connectivity is also likely to play a significant role in shaping the future, offering a more efficient, safe and environment-friendly transportation option.

## Electric Vehicles

The trend towards electrification is driven by the need to reduce emissions, improve energy security and enhance sustainability. In the coming years, we can expect to see significant growth in the number of EVs on the road, as well as the expansion of charging infrastructure and the introduction of new models. The integration of advanced technologies such as autonomous driving, connectivity and artificial intelligence is also expected to play a significant role in shaping the future of EVs, offering a more convenient and efficient driving experience. Most notable advances in EVs include the adoption of newer battery technologies (beyond lithium-ion), fast wireless charging technologies, electrified roads (possibly using overhead cables), battery swapping and development of ultra-fast chargers.

## Rise of End-to-End Automotive Platforms

Vehicles of the future will soon be like supercomputers on wheels as the sector is fast moving away from being hardware-defined to a software-defined mobility platform. To successfully equip a vehicle with the latest features such as onboard infotainment, electrification, self-driving abilities, and advanced driver assistance systems, it is now critical for automakers to possess better quality software systems ensuring seamless integration among vehicle subsystems and security systems. It is estimated that software complexity in vehicles is on track to nearly triple over the next ten years.

## Smart Manufacturing and Repair

The automotive industry has been the most enthusiastic to adopt smart factories and has undertaken remarkable investments to propagate digital manufacturing operations. It is also second in line to use additive manufacturing for production. Digital twin, where manufacturers can optimize every phase of their production process, and AR, which assists in optimizing the assembly process (making it quicker and reducing errors), ensure a safe environment for workers and reduce the cost of manufacturing. Incorporating AR has allowed automotive technicians to perform complex vehicle repairs and maintenance more accurately and quickly.

—**Aashish Mehra**
Chief Research Officer
MarketsandMarkets

# 1

# Flying New Frontiers

The final frontier is vast. As commercial space flights gain momentum, other planets appear closer than ever.

Emerging technology is helping leverage space for various terrestrial uses. It is also helping scientists, researchers and entrepreneurs reduce project time and cost. Two critical shifts are propelling the space industry: the miniaturization of satellites and the use of AI for understanding the dynamics of the universe.

In the space-tech category, many startups and legacy companies are putting their efforts to reduce the size of satellites. Smaller satellites orbit closer to the earth and are more flexible than larger ones. Proximity to earth means that the transmission time of data to the base station is faster. Consequently, the energy required to run such satellites is lower. As camera technology has also miniaturized, these satellites can take much better photos of earth with a higher resolution than the large satellites that orbit much higher. Usually, such satellites are launched as a cluster with varying objectives. As the cost is lower, they can be replaced easily or their software updated more efficiently. Smarter algorithms allow the operators to coordinate the activities within the satellite clusters.

According to an assessment, the new space industry is composed of more than a thousand companies worldwide. Small satellite constellation architectures, reusable launch vehicles, space travel and other technologies have attracted new investors into this industry.

The next deep shift is the use of AI and machine learning (ML) to understand the data being generated by satellites and terrestrial observatories. While scientists and astronomers are constantly trying to make sense of space phenomena and events, it can take months and even years to understand spatial activities. However, algorithms can be trained to understand signals and analyse different types of light generated by stars and planets. Researchers say that the accuracy of reading the data with AI and ML can be more than 90 per cent, often higher than that by humans, and in lesser time.

The Vera Rubin Observatory in Chile, expected to become operational in 2023, will use a 3200-megapixel camera to observe the night skies. It will photograph the entire sky every night and store over eighty terabytes of images every time. Over a period of ten years, the car-sized camera of the observatory will capture sixty petabytes of data.

No single scientist or team can analyse or understand this data without the help of trained algorithms. AI and ML will scour through the stream of valuable images and related data to make sense of the constantly changing universe, which is impacting our lives.

Against this background, policymakers, entrepreneurs and scientists are collaborating at various levels to deepen their knowledge of space. Many startups are at the leading edge of using emerging technology for space exploration and knowledge generation. The use of such technologies will be unique, especially with the opening up of geospatial mapping for the private sector in many countries.

## Space Systems and Space Exploration

In general, space-exploration technologies are expected to have much more advancements in the next few decades than it has had in the entire human history. In an interview with the World Economic Forum, George Whitesides, chief executive officer at Virgin Galactic and cochair of the Global Future Council on Space Technologies, said, 'Space technologies help us understand our mothership. The climate, peace and security and energy issues of the earth.'[1]

The space exploration industry has been systematically reshaping itself with fundamental digital tools such as robotics, additive manufacturing/3D printing, augmented reality and big data analytics. AI and blockchain are strengthening security and management solutions using the data generated by space businesses. The industry is also embracing advancements such as integrated computer vision, voice recognition technology, advanced augmented reality and high-performance space suits using Digital Thread.[2]

Today there are *mega-constellations* of low earth orbit satellites that aim to provide advanced global connectivity. Mega-constellations are satellite groups that enhance the efficiency, capacity and safety of a wide range of earth-based services and businesses. These include the maritime, energy, banking, government and telecommunications sectors. In a recent article, Dylan Taylor, chairman and CEO of Voyager Space Holdings, and a veteran of the space industry, said that in the next five to twenty years, satellite mega-constellations, fast point-to-point suborbital transport (saving fuel emissions) and asteroid impact prevention (though the technology is still in its infancy) will make their mark.

Other major innovations from the leading organizations in the aerospace and defence industry include the following:

## Lockheed Martin's Digital Tapestry

Under its digital transformation programme, Lockheed Martin, a global security and aerospace company, has created a digital tapestry environment to design and produce parts and systems that would have been impossible using traditional design and manufacturing techniques. It is supported by a gamut of digital systems including state-of-the-art information technologies, advanced manufacturing techniques, 3D modelling, virtual reality simulation, big data analytics, additive manufacturing and automated inspection and testing.

## Blue Origin Federation

Owned by Jeff Bezos, Blue Origin has developed the fully reusable New Shepard suborbital rocket system. Suborbital space flights will allow civilians to experience weightlessness and see the curvature of the earth. Blue Origin has also started registration for seats.[3]

## Space Tourism

SpaceX, Blue Origin and Virgin Galactic will soon take humans to space, with customers ranging from governments to space tourists, and some day settlers and colonists too.

These innovations will also ensure a wide range of benefits for the earth—from a better understanding of climate to ubiquitous broadband. While meteorological satellites have been used for a long time to forecast extreme weather events, the onset of Space 2.0 will ensure a better understanding of critical issues including ways to combat climate change, tackle wildlife crime with AI cameras and even improve agriculture. For example, the International Co-operation for Animal Research Using Space (ICARUS) initiative is using a satellite on the International Space Station to create an 'internet of animals'.

## New Space Economy

In the coming years, there will be an increase in public and private initiatives in space exploration with a converging global interest in moon exploration. Reports suggest that in the period from 2019 to 2029, the global government investment in space transportation will reach US$121 billion.[4]

In terms of applications, moon and Mars explorations are expected to account for the majority of space missions to be launched by 2027, as lunar exploration becomes the focus of private and public stakeholders. A total of eighteen missions are anticipated to be launched for other deep space exploration, while the remaining missions will be dedicated to Mars exploration.

In August 2019, SpaceX (US) announced its plan to launch a low-cost small satellite into the earth's orbit. Other launch providers such as Arianespace SA (France), Indian Space

Research Organization and various semi-commercial ventures in China have also developed programmes for dedicated and ride-share launches for small satellites.

Privatization is expected to promote new entrants in satellite and satellite launch vehicle manufacturing. Growth in the number of launch vehicles will, in turn, lead to an increase in the number of satellite launches. A larger number of satellites in the earth's orbit will enable satellite data or imagery service providers to target a broader customer base.

The growth of entrepreneurship in the space industry has been encouraged by privatization in countries and regions, such as the US, Canada, China and Europe. For instance, the launch of a space surveillance satellite by Canada has enabled several private companies in the country to offer space surveillance services. Several companies, including Planet Labs, Inc. (US), ICEYE (Finland) and Spire Global, Inc. (US), are operating in both upstream and downstream markets. This ensures that the earth observation's downstream market yields more commercial results due to its wide variety of applications. The upstream market, however, remains favourable for governments as it enables agencies such as the European Space Agency (ESA) to provide free satellite imagery data to various institutions and organizations.

Furthermore, in an age of instant information, connectivity must be effective, affordable and always available. Especially when IoT is connecting billions of devices and 'sensorizing' almost everything—from pipelines to assembly lines to logistics to consumer electronics. As sensors actively transmit data across systems, the biggest need of the hour is speed, quality and affordability of connectivity. Since most retail consumers are dependent on mobile service providers for connectivity, cellular networks will choke as devices begin to ride their bandwidth.

Moreover, cellular networks work best in urban areas but are not as effective in the rest of the places.

IoT is increasingly shifting to satellite-based connectivity solutions. The world's largest connectivity providers are now focusing on IoT solutions. These include Iridium, OrbComm, Inmarsat, Globalstar and Vodafone IoT. In some ways, the satellite broadcast revolution, which beamed TV signals to hundreds of millions of homes over the last few decades, is now moving to the IoT.

Satellite IoT has become a strong market segment in itself. 'Satellite IoT services are very helpful for a mobile network to expand beyond the limitations of terrestrial networks. Deep sea, remote and mining regions are just a few examples of places where satellite connection enables IoT systems,' says a report by Douglas Insights.

The satellite IoT market is estimated to grow at CAGR of approximately 20 per cent during 2021–28, from $850 million to $6 billion, according to Douglas Insights.[5]

A shift within this market is towards small satellite constellations. On 6 January 2020, Elon Musk-promoted SpaceX launched its third batch of 60 Starlink satellites. Apart from IoT, Musk's objective is to revolutionize the world's internet connectivity by taking it to the remotest of locations with a constellation of thousands of satellites. In a filing with Federal Communications Commission (FCC) of the US, SpaceX said: 'The system is designed to provide a wide range of broadband and communications services for residential, commercial, institutional, government and professional users worldwide.'[6]

In 2019, Swarm Technologies received approval from the Federal Communications Commission, the US regulator, to launch sixty miniature satellites to create an ever-present network and connectivity for devices across the world.[7] As per NSR, 'Small satellite IoT constellations will disrupt the market in the longer term. Lower cost satellite architectures, with a lower total cost of ownership for end users, will drive new customers to these services.'

Satellites bring connectivity to virtually every part of the world. This has important implications for the logistics, shipping and transportation sectors. Even when they are in locations that have no cellular connectivity, ships, trains and trucks can remain connected to their organizations.

However, the cost of satellite-based connectivity is still not affordable for many companies. One kilobyte of data can cost a dollar while for cellular services, it is a fraction. As an answer to the issue, a Silicon Valley startup by an Indian technologist is offering an affordable solution. Parth Trivedi, CEO and cofounder of Skylo Technologies, has developed low-cost hardware and solutions which are ideal for Indian and emerging market conditions. Skylo has converted a satellite-receiver dish into a printed circuit board-based device combined with IoT connectivity.

Low-cost, high-speed and ever-present connectivity can soon be a reality with new satellite technologies that are rapidly changing the communications sector. Both government services and enterprises in India can benefit from such breakthroughs as most of the country gets connected with satellite IoT.

## Sustainable Air Mobility

Recovering from the COVID-19 pandemic slump, the commercial air space is already showing positive signs and is growing at a substantial rate. According to Airbus CEO Guillaume Faury, 'The year [2021] had significant orders from airlines worldwide, showing confidence in the sustainable growth of air travel post-COVID-19.'[8] The aerospace and defence sector, whereas, remained insulated from the global impact of COVID-19 with investments and budgets staying strong consistently. Although the industry growth numbers remained positive, the sector remains one of the highest contributors towards global warming, and one of the most challenging sectors to decarbonize. According to a report by Boston Consulting Group, the global defence industry's contribution to worldwide $CO_2$ emissions could soar from 2 per cent in 2021 to 25 per cent by 2050, unless there is aggressive work done to reduce the carbon footprint.[9] Similarly, a report from Deloitte highlights that a return flight from London to New York City generates over 1 tonne of carbon dioxide per passenger, which is close to what an average citizen in a developing country would produce per year.[10]

With the commitment to net-zero emission goals, the aerospace and defence sector too is relying heavily on technological innovations and digitization to reduce its emission levels with improved operational efficiency. Advanced military capabilities, innovative space technology and advanced air mobility (AAM) are some of the key technology highlights working towards reducing the impact on the environment. It is also rapidly moving towards either electrification or alternate fuel options. Over the years, the sector has already transitioned towards paperless maintenance, virtual inspections, predictive analytics, augmented reality/virtual reality (AR/VR) solutions and a series of innovative technologies to improve customer experience. The defence and aerospace companies are set to embrace digital thread technology and smart factories widely to achieve better visibility of critical material and component supply. Sensors and data analytics are being increasingly used to assess structural health through a non-destructive evaluation system.

In research conducted by Accenture on the digital revolution of the aerospace and defence space, 97 per cent of the participants (executives of aerospace and defence companies) said their organizations were innovating with utmost urgency and call to action.[11] It is clear that the industry is not just competing for a share of the market but also working diligently towards creating new genres of competitive and sustainable technology stacks to tap into the full spectrum of tech offerings. In the survey, 81 per cent of the participants agreed that business and technology strategies are now inseparable.

## Advanced Air Mobility

The AAM and net zero aviation remain the focus of the commercial aviation space today. Keeping customer experience at the core, commercial aviation space has been harnessing the power of innovative technologies such as robotics, IoT, AI, biometrics, blockchain, wearables and more. Electric flying vehicles are the highlight of future air mobility (FAM).

According to McKinsey data, 2021 was a record year for FAM. Research experts from McKinsey note that electric flying vehicles will be a safe, affordable and sustainable mode of transportation, and become a reality very soon. It will also be a viable alternative to traditional taxis. Daniel Wiegand, CEO of air-mobility company Lilium, believes that electric passenger aircraft will be commonplace by 2030. While Florian Reuter, CEO of Bruchsal-based aircraft manufacturer Volocopter says, 'In 30 years, AAM will be as ubiquitous as any other transportation mode.' Over 250 businesses worldwide are working towards manufacturing, building and operating air taxis in the next five years.[12] A McKinsey survey was conducted to understand customer acceptance of electric vertical take-off and landing aircraft (eVTOLs). It found that India and Brazil were among the most willing countries to pay for future flying-taxi offerings.[13] Initially, these vehicles would be driven by pilots but in the long term, it is envisaged that they will fly autonomously.

Hyundai has described the US-based Supernal as a spinoff company that will take the lead in developing the conglomerate's first family of eVTOL. Intel, in association with Volocopter, conducted the first run-through of its two-seater eighteen-rotor air taxi in 2018. It took off in North America despite a few dry runs in Dubai. The air taxi was operated by a pilot and used batteries for power. It could fly for thirty minutes with a maximum range of seventeen miles.

Reuters reported that in November 2022, 'the Volocopter test aircraft, which resembles a large drone with eight rotors, took off with a passenger on board from the Pontoise–Cormeilles airfield outside Paris and briefly circled around while other aircraft were in the vicinity.'

Volocopter CEO Dirk Hoke said that in the next eighteen months, it will prepare its craft for certification and said he hopes to launch short commercial flights by 2024, when Paris holds the Summer Olympic Games.[14]

The aerial ride-sharing companies' end-use segment is likely to witness a heavy boost during the forecast period owing to a large number of helicopters and on-demand air taxis, and the expected increase in the adoption of on-demand air taxis for intracity travel post-2025.

The ride-sharing companies' end-use market is projected to grow from US$1.6 billion in 2021 to US$4.6 billion by 2030, at a compound annual growth rate of 12 per cent from 2021 to 2030.

## Sustainable Aviation with Alternate Fuels

Urban air mobility is also focusing on the development of alternative aviation fuel, mainly hydrogen, which can be the key to sustainable air travel and will contribute immensely to the industry's emissions-reduction strategy. According to Grazia Vitaldini, chief technology officer at Airbus, 'Hydrogen is one of the most promising technology vectors to allow the basic human need for mobility in better harmony with our environment.'[15] The unique attributes of hydrogen, such as easy availability globally, safety, reduced emissions and lightweightness, make it an ideal fuel. ZeroAvia, a California-based startup, is developing aircraft with a hydrogen-electric (fuel cell) powertrain, which will be able to carry up to twenty passengers to about 350 nautical miles (648 km). The mission is supported by the UK government in partnership with private investors and commercial bodies. According to reports, ZeroAvia is currently working on bringing to market a zero-emission system capable of flying twenty-seat aircraft 300 nautical miles by 2025.

This opens up the possibility of green air travel from Birmingham to destinations such as Edinburgh, Glasgow, Aberdeen, Belfast, Isle of Man and Dublin by the middle of this decade. ZeroAvia is aiming to get an emissions-free eighty-seat aircraft flying up to 1,000 nautical miles by 2027.[16]

In a blog statement in February 2023, the company said, 'Last month ZeroAvia flew a 19-seat Dornier 228, the largest commercial aircraft powered by hydrogen fuel cell to date. This was a significant step forward for the decarbonization of aviation, in time for getting to the UN's net zero 2050 goal.'[17]

The hydrogen aircraft market is projected to reach US$7.4 billion by 2030. Recent technological advancements in propulsion systems, fuel cells, fuel efficiency, cryogenic storage, hydrogen fuel extraction and aircraft structural design specifically for hydrogen-powered aircraft have driven the market.

The aviation industry has made steady improvements in fuel efficiency over time. However, the gains have been overpowered by the tremendous rise in air traffic. In the coming future, along with efficiency, the aviation industry will need to make substantial efforts towards decarbonization through innovative ways. The task is not limited to airlines and their original equipment manufacturers (OEMs). It also includes the larger ecosystem of air mobility including startups and investors.[18]

## Sustainable Aviation with Electric Aircrafts

The goal to achieve sustainability in aviation driven by consumers and regulators is making notable transformations in a sector considered to be a huge consumer of fossil fuels. About 45 per cent of the operating cost incurred by an airline is the cost of fuel. Fuel costs are volatile as they are affected by various economic and geopolitical factors. Domestic airlines in the US incur a cost of up to US$5 billion per month on fuel. For airline operators, reducing operational costs matters more than ever because increasingly the air passenger is leaning towards the price. The four major ways through which the aviation industry is trying to move towards sustainability are using sustainable fuels (SAF), electrification of aircraft, using hydrogen-powered aircraft and deploying efficient aircraft on short routes.

The latest developments in electric and electronic aircraft technologies offer significant opportunities to electric aircraft as well as component manufacturers. Aircraft manufacturers are examining ways to generate and distribute large power that will be sufficient to carry an aircraft over long distances. High-energy density batteries, high-performance electric motors, distributed architectures and power electronics (in the starter/ generation system of the main engine) are some of the upcoming technologies for aircraft.

To achieve stringent emission targets, electric airplanes are providing the scale of transformation required, and many companies are racing to develop them. Electric propulsion motors would not only eliminate direct carbon emissions, but also reduce fuel costs by up to 90 per cent, maintenance by up to 50 per cent and noise by nearly 70 per cent.

Among the companies working on the electric flight are Airbus, Ampaire, MagniX and Eviation. All these companies are flight-testing aircraft meant for private, corporate or commuter trips, and are seeking certification from the US Federal Aviation Administration. Cape Air, one of the largest regional airlines, expects to be among the first customers and plans to buy the Alice nine-passenger electric aircraft from Eviation.

The electric aircraft market is expected to reach US$27.6 billion by 2030 driven by the development of unmanned aerial vehicles (UAVs) and eVTOLs, which are the key factors driving the electric aircraft market.

Sustainable aviation is projected to lead the market in the short term with an opportunity of US$15.7 billion in 2030 driven by the increasing demand and obligations of the aviation industry to reduce greenhouse gas emissions.

Biofuel will be another major sustainable aviation fuel type that will be used by the aviation industry because it can be blended with gasoline and will not require a substantial reworking of current aircraft/engine designs.

## Advanced Military Capabilities

Aero-defence technologies are bringing in several spectacular changes with fighter jets. Today, there are jets that can shoot high-powered lasers, robots that can mine hours of intelligence data in milliseconds and tactical aircraft that can think for themselves, as well as electric military aircraft with similar capabilities.

In November 2022, the US Air Force used electric flying cars. 'The Lift HEXA, an electric vertical takeoff and landing aircraft, lifted off at Duke Field Nov. 16 for a routine flight, only this sortie was piloted by Airmen,' said a statement by Elgin Airforce Base. 'For the first time here, Airmen remotely controlled the aircraft during multiple takeoffs, flights and landings. This was an early step in creating a training program to incorporate Airmen into the aircraft's flight operations.'

eVTOLs are part of a large effort called Agility Prime by the USAF.

Agility Prime is the US Air Force's transformative vertical lift programme that is partnering with the eVTOL commercial industry to propel the third revolution in aerospace and start to field a new class of air mobility systems.[19]

'Our big focus this year that we need to do for the program is get some of the piloted and larger platforms out in the hands of our test professionals,' Lt Col. Thomas Meagher, AFWERX Prime division chief, told *Air and Space Forces* magazine. 'You can get these things into exercises and see what they can do, which serves two purposes: One, it informs us for those use cases … but then, two, it also shows others what they are capable of, which will, in turn, inform Air Force and DOD decisions.' Among eVTOL milestones reached in 2022, Joby Aviation scored a high-altitude mark of more than 11,000 feet and a speed of more than 200 mph. The company previously received approval for military airworthiness.[20]

Another key invention is electric short take-off and landing aircraft (eSTOL) that utilizes battery technology and attains propulsive power from electricity. These aircraft are meant to take off and land on shorter runways.[21] In early 2022, the US Air

Force awarded a Phase III Small Business Innovation Research (SBIR) contract to Electra.aero, Inc. to support the development of its eSTOL aircraft. The eSTOL aircraft are designed with distributed electric propulsion and will have the capacity to transport nine passengers, or up to 816.4 kg of cargo, within a range of 804.6 km. These aircraft are designed to greatly reduce noise emissions as compared to traditional helicopters. eSTOLs do not require a new on-ground charging infrastructure to support their operations as they will have an inbuilt compact turbine-powered generator to recharge the batteries mid-flight.

Another major technology breakthrough in the segment is the introduction of automatic air-to-air refuelling, between an aerial tanker and a fighter aircraft.[22] Aerial refuelling or air-to-air refuelling and tanking is a system in which fuel is transferred from one military tanker aircraft to another military aircraft, fixed-wing jets and helicopters. While air-to-air refuelling is not new, Airbus in October 2022 announced the world's first fully automatic air-to-air refuelling operation. Technologies used in automatic refuelling include image processing, visual tracking algorithm, drones and new video-based technologies.[23] Aerial refuelling expands the range of an aircraft in air and saves time as the aircraft does not have to land to refuel.[24]

Today, defence and commercial vessels are also armed with advanced systems that ensure higher safety and efficiency levels. These ships integrate varied systems and subsystems, and enable effective decision-making. They use sensor fusion technology and AI, which allows for reduction or complete elimination of human intervention. The rise of this remotely operated segment of the integrated marine automation system is an outcome of increased investments in unmanned operations. At the same time, the demand for electronic warfare systems is also expected to be driven up by three main aspects: rapid technological advancements, rising focus on directed energy weapons and the increasing need for electronic protection prowess in armed forces worldwide.[25]

## Digital Battlefields

The AI and IoT have emerged as complementary technologies that are finding significant applications in digital battlefield products for military exercises and critical missions. The constantly expanding network infrastructure along with the increasing usage of electronic military devices in the defence sector worldwide would invariably require AI for categorizing, processing, fusing and analysing the big data generated. The data produced from digital battlefield devices and related sensors would be heterogeneous in nature and require AI for analysis. AI systems, when merged with IoT, would be especially useful in regulating digital battlefield products including military devices by analysing their transmitted data, and controlling their operations to match user requirements. They can also coordinate and synchronize digital battlefield products with other devices used in combat operations, and efficiently modify their outputs.

The military is generating large amounts of data owing to the increasing usage of sensors for drones, telemetry, airborne surveillance, connected reconnaissance tools and other military applications. The data generated plays a vital role in improving the deployment of assets and soldiers in the battle space. Big data also plays a crucial function in countering border security threats and terrorism across the globe. The growing tension and conflict between neighbouring countries is forcing them to focus on enhancing their capabilities through advanced technologies including big data analytics. High-value data is generated and collected by a variety of nodes in the connected military network and analysed by advanced data analytic tools to enhance the critical missions of the military forces. The increasing use of connected devices for military applications and deployed unmanned systems requires the substantial use of big data analytics to sift through the data generated. Advanced analytics or big data analytics is a vital tool for the armed forces during combat operations on the battlefield and for counter-terrorism operations. It can help tackle enemies on a global scale and decrease operational risk by increasing the capability and safety of the armed forces. Advanced analytics can improve live combat operations by enhancing the ability to assess, assimilate and act on these insights and provide operational intelligence to save soldiers' lives.

The global digital battlefield market analysis consists of components, technology, platform, applications and regions. Based on technology, the digital battlefield market is segmented into AI, 3D printing, IoT, big data analytics, robotic process automation, cloud computing and master data management, digital twin, smart sensors, blockchain, AR and VR, and 5G. Digital battlefield products and systems embedded with such technologies are finding growing use in warfighting applications involving human–machine collaboration and combat teams. Militaries across the world are adopting digital battlefield products and systems to improve the performance of personnel in networked battle scenarios.

The IoT in the digital battlefield market is expected to be worth US$24.3 billion by 2025 according to MarketsandMarkets. The 5G segment is expected to be worth US$3.582 billion by 2025. The IoT technology used in digital battlefield products and services comprises a network of sensors and military devices that are interconnected by using cloud and edge computing technologies. Such a network also helps increase situational awareness, enables risk assessment and reduces response time. The interconnected devices include soldier systems, military equipment and other unmanned vehicles with sensors that continuously collect data to obtain useful intelligence during critical missions.

The adoption of AI for critical decision-making in the battlefield is set to replace the traditional human military commanders in the coming future. The Defense Advanced Research Projects Agency has initiated a programme that has introduced AI for the decision-making process, thus removing the need for human intervention.

In a nutshell, aerospace and defence are at a juncture where they are navigating their organizations into the future, combating disruption and embracing opportunities powered by emerging digital and electric technologies. But the industry needs to digitize across the value chain and automate it. It needs to embrace new business models to be able to address the shifting demands and focus these. Finally, it needs to be open to collaboration for effective innovation and work with peers, partners, suppliers and vendors to sustain and grow business value.

## Novel Drone Applications

The increasing use of drones in various civil and commercial applications due to their superior endurance, low operation costs and enhanced payload capabilities has resulted in their increased production and the growth of the market. The transformation is required in the three segments of drone usage: mobility, delivery and services.

## Rise of Drone Deliveries

With urban mobility rapidly evolving, the drone delivery industry is already a reality and booming. According to McKinsey, drones could become an important part of the delivery supply chain. In early 2022, more than 2,000 commercial drone deliveries were occurring every day worldwide, and that number has only grown since. While it is still small relative to the total number of commercial deliveries, it indicates that current activity involves more than just test-flights. Drone technology has the potential to meet a range of last-mile consumer-use cases, such as prepared food, convenience products and other small packages, as well as B2B needs, such as moving medical samples to labs.

If drone operators can eventually manage twenty drones simultaneously, our analysis, using reasonable assumptions, suggests that a single package delivery will cost about $1.50 to $2. That is in line with the per-package cost for an electric car delivering five packages, and any type of van delivering 100 packages in a milk-run format when a driver delivers all packages in a single trip—a process which is not always feasible, McKinsey says.[26]

Walmart's drone-delivery programme has completed its intended expansion plans for 2022. The company now operates, with its vendors, thirty-six drone delivery hubs across seven states, including Arizona, Arkansas, Florida, North Carolina, Texas, Utah and Virginia. According to Walmart, it has safely completed more than 6,000 deliveries to customers in as little as thirty minutes.[27]

Amazon is rolling out its drone-delivery plan as well. It has completed its first drone deliveries, with small packages of up to 2.2 kg to homes in Texas and California. Through its Prime Air subsidiary, Amazon has been delivering to homes in College Station, Texas, and Lockeford, California, with more locations soon to come online with a target of delivering to homes less than sixty minutes after ordering.[28]

'We like to refer to the drone as being independently safe, which means that it has the power to make the decision. It saw something that had a heat signature underneath the drone and was able to not deliver a package and return back to the station. But the drones do have an operator in command that is overseeing the entire airspace,' says Calsee Hendrickson, who leads product and programme management for the Prime Air drone programme.[29]

Autonomous flight systems will be the future of the aerospace industry and take on many forms—from drones to space vehicles.

## Shift in Business Models

Drone inspection and monitoring will lead to disruption in the conventional maintenance, repair and overhaul business from 2021 to 2030. Due to their benefits, including timeliness and cost-effective data acquisition, drones have been comprehensively exploited by various industries. The conventional data collection technique is restricted by time and safety, often leading to a shortage of detailed information for monitoring and evaluation purposes. Rather than conventional human, airplane or helicopter methods, nowadays organizations benefit from both previously unavailable levels of visibility and reasonable cost by using drones for inspection and monitoring purposes. The usage of drones helps improve worker protection and provides access to information on assets in numerous dynamic and challenging industries. Drones reduce the risks for inspectors, decrease downtime and provide accurate data on an asset's life history. Compared to humans, drones can reduce inspection time and cost by up to 70 per cent.

These UAVs can be sent to hazardous places where conventional equipment cannot reach. The type of UAVs employed for such applications depends on the size of the area to be covered. Fixed-wing UAVs are used for mapping large areas whereas rotary-wing UAVs offer accurate data on the landscape and are primarily used for inspection.

A large number of mining companies are employing drones that are equipped with digital cameras. These remotely operated small aircraft produce high-resolution aerial images that are further processed to produce 3D models and orthophotos. Surveyors and engineers make use of the data obtained from 3D models to forecast the development of mines and calculate volumes of stockpiles. A drone can provide important data about the state of the aboveground area of mines, thereby ensuring the safety of mine workers.

## Summary

The flights of fancy are here. And they are getting fancier. Despite all the constrains and restrictions, flying will remain critical for trans-continental passenger movement. With a combination of new technologies that improve safety and fuel efficiency, aviation could see fundamental shifts to electricity. Defence and aerospace have always been ahead of other industries. Use of renewable and green fuels is driving the next level of industrial revolution in the sector. Many technologies used by consumers and civil society were born in the satellite of the defence sector. This pace will only accelerate in the future.

# 2

# Planting in Air, Earth and Water

So far, the drones that were considered important for the agriculture sector were nature-made winged insects. They were a key component of the bee-based natural pollination cycle. The new age drone is a whirring machine with rotors that can help farmers plan, grow and manage their crops.

For the farm sector in India, which has had low levels of mechanization, the impact of drones can be tremendous. Drones can help it leapfrog to modernization in the same way that mobile phones helped India overcome its traditional lack of connectivity. A report by World Economic Forum's Centre for the Fourth Industrial Revolution emphasizes this perspective.[1] It says that the use of drones in agriculture can create a US$100 billion gross domestic product (GDP) boost and help millions get

better livelihood: 'Drones are poised to be an effective tool to
support farmers reduce their operating costs and efforts, while
at the same time optimizing their input use. There are multiple
uses for drones, including surveying, seeding, spraying  and
pollination that are at different stages of technology and business
model maturity.'

There are several areas where drones are making their
presence felt. These include seed propagation, pesticide
spraying, yield prediction, land records, insurance assessment
and crop monitoring.

Several policies of the government are now promoting the
manufacture and use of drones in not just the agriculture sector
but the others. For instance, a mission on agri-mechanization
will support the use of drones while the Drone Shakti
programme is promoting drone-as-a-service across the country.
The Production Linked Incentive scheme and export promotion
incentives are expected to bring US$50 billion of investment in
drone production.

Krishi Vigyan Kendras (KVK) under the Indian Council of
Agriculture Research have been working in the fields with
farmers to educate and propagate the use of drones. As knowledge
and resource centres, they have run pilot projects in Kerala for
pesticide spraying with surprisingly positive results. Another KVK
in Tamil Nadu bought a drone for field trials and demonstrated
unprecedented efficiency. A drone with the capacity to carry up
to ten litres of pesticide can cover thirty acres per day. According
to reports, the trials have revealed that the drone could complete
spraying pesticides in a few hours, which would have otherwise
taken two farm labourers more than a day.[2] Not just drones, but a
host of innovations are changing agriculture in India in irreversible
ways.

## Food and Agriculture

From agriculture to storage to transportation and evolving customer preferences, the industry is working stringently to introduce solutions backed by new-age technology. Ingenious techniques such as indoor and vertical farming, precision farming, livestock technology and modern greenhouse practice are redefining the entire agri space meticulously. The collective goal is to boost the food value chain from production to last-mile delivery while ensuring minimum impact on the environment and minimizing wastage.

According to the UN projections, the world's population is expected to be 9.7 billion by 2050.[3]

As per the Food and Agriculture Organization, to meet the subsequent rise in demand for food and to serve the nutritional requirements of the population, the agricultural sector will need to push itself by at least 70 per cent compared to the current production standards. However, a rampant intensification of agricultural activities and food production will only prove to be detrimental to the environment that is already coping with threatening climatic conditions and rapidly deteriorating weather patterns. To meet the massive rise in resource consumption while ensuring environmental sustainability, the food and beverage industry is consistently innovating and shifting towards newer forms of production.

According to MarketsandMarkets, food and agriculture technology and products market is projected to grow from US$494.9 billion in 2018 to US$729.5 billion by 2023, at a CAGR of 8.1 per cent during the forecast period. The growth is largely attributed to the increase in demand and consumption of livestock-based products and seafood, rise in consumer awareness about food safety, governments' support to adopt modern agricultural techniques and demand for agricultural production due to the increasing population.

A deep dive into the advancements in the sector—from farm to fork and how the future looks—will help us understand the opportunities, challenges and new business models that define the segment today.

## Agriculture Is Now Smart Farming

Agriculture has transformed into a technologically intense and data-rich industry with the advent of advancements such as guidance systems, variable rate technology, IoT, AI, and remote sensing. Thus, now we call it smart farming—it is all about increasing profitability while enhancing sustainability and preserving the environment by minimizing the use of water, fertilizers and energy. The COVID-19 pandemic has further accelerated the adoption of technology and digital solutions in every industry by many folds and farming is no exception, even though the agriculture sector has been a late entrant.

Over the last ten years, agricultural technology has seen a huge growth in investment—close to US$9 billion—globally.[4] This has bolstered new tech adoption, making it possible for the producers to grow more with less land, water other natural resources, as well as less human workforce. Some of the prominent technologies gaining momentum in the agricultural sector are as follows:

## Blockchain

Especially for the livestock farming sector, blockchain is creating an efficient supply chain that allows to trace products and improve transactional efficiencies. It has already begun to positively impact the meat industry in many ways. Although a nascent technology, blockchain could be a game changer by enhancing the ease and flexibility in farm management as well as transparency in the supply chain. A research by MarketsandMarkets[5] reveals that the global blockchain in agriculture and food supply chain market size estimated at US$133 million in 2020 will grow to US$948 million by 2025. Blockchain farming has the ability to mitigate counterfeits in agri-food production and supply chains. It ensures better handling and presents healthier products to consumers, generating trust with business players. Stakeholders are increasingly demanding the need to trace and track raw materials to increase trust in the value chain.

## Internet of Things

The IoT technology, on the other hand, forms the core of smart farming. At present, precision farming has become one of the most significant applications of IoT technology, whereby farmers can use various software and hardware devices to collect farm-related data that can help them in better decision-making and boost the productivity of their lands and crops. As per MarketsandMarkets Research, the precision farming market is expected to grow from US$8.5 billion in 2022 to US$15.6 billion by 2030, at a CAGR of 7.9 per cent. The IoT has further bolstered innovations such as automated control systems, variable rate technology, farm robots and autonomous farm vehicles. It is being utilized in agricultural drones, with sensors for imaging, mapping and surveying of fields. Other areas benefiting greatly from the IoT include greenhouses, indoor farming and livestock monitoring. The IoT tags in livestock not only track the movement of farm animals but also capture and send information about animal health and behaviour.

## Artificial Intelligence

The AI can process weather, soil, moisture and temperature data together to help farmers in better decision-making. In indoor farming applications, AI is utilized in robotics for maximum space optimization while moving pots and plants. It can also help create seasonal forecasting models to improve crop productivity. For livestock, AI systems can deliver the exact quantity of feed required depending on the growth stage of farm animals. The overall AI in the agriculture market is expected to grow from US$1 billion in 2020 to US$4 billion by 2026.

### Image Processing with Artificial Intelligence

Image processing is largely used in AI-driven software and hardware applications. For instance, in drones, AI is used to process multispectral images to monitor crop health or detect the spread of pests. Blue River Technology (a subsidiary of John Deere) uses machine learning (ML) to apply herbicides autonomously and accurately. Various agricultural robots for fruit-picking, seeding, weed removal, pesticide spraying and surveying developed at present are being integrated with image-processing technology. AI is being programmed to differentiate between fruits, weeds and other plants using machine-learning technology. Real-time data management and monitoring software used in agriculture also rely heavily on AI.

### Drones or Unmanned Aerial Vehicles

These are now a common technology in the agriculture space. The advancement in unmanned aerial vehicle's capabilities and its integration with AI technology has made precision farming a reality. With a combination of global positioning system, photogrammetry and Light Detection and Ranging cameras mounted on small UAVs, the large amounts of photos collected automatically get analysed by the AI software and get stitched together to give an accurate 3D rendering of the landscape. These applications are critical in surveying and providing data to assist farmers in decisions regarding the productive placement of crops and water catchment areas. Drones can send all the required imagery wirelessly after completing their flight.

According to a recent IDTechEx report,[6] the six major areas that will have the biggest impact on the industry backed by IoT, AI, ML and blockchain are small autonomous robots, intelligent tractor-pull implements, robotic implements with simple vision/ control, autonomous tractors, autonomous sprayers and fresh fruit picking.

These will further lead to newer business models disrupting the basic premise of farming for the better. According to research by the McKinsey Center for Advanced Connectivity and the McKinsey Global Institute, agriculture is just one of the seven sectors that, fuelled by advanced connectivity, will contribute US\$2 trillion to US\$3 trillion in additional value to global GDP over the next decade.[7]

## Next Frontiers in Agriculture: Vertical Farming

Due to industrial development and urbanization, we are losing arable lands every day. In 2015, scientists reported that the earth has lost a third of its arable lands over the past forty years. Increasing food demand along with ever-decreasing arable lands poses one of the greatest challenges facing us. However, the innovation of vertical farming is gradually proving itself to be the precise solution to this issue. Vertical farming has many advantages over traditional farming methods. Crops can now be grown irrespective of climatic conditions, land or water issues or even labour shortages.

Vertical farming produces more food per square metre. To accomplish this, crops are cultivated in stacked layers in a tower-like structure. Additionally, a combination of natural and artificial lights is used to maintain the perfect brightness level in the room. Technologies such as rotating beds are used to improve lighting efficiency. Coconut husks and similar non-soil mediums are common features of vertical farming. Various sustainable features of vertical farming are offsetting the energy cost of farming.

Studies show that vertical farms use up to 70 per cent less water than traditional farms,[8] which is a critical feature in drought-prone zones. This is common with either hydroponic technology, where vegetables are grown in a nutrient-dense bowl of water, or aeroponic methods, where the plant roots are systematically sprayed with water and nutrients and use artificial grow lights in place of natural sunlight or even aquaponics.

In addition to mechanisms such as hydroponics, aeroponics and aquaponics, vegetables are being grown differently in building-based, shipping container-based and deep farms. Among all the methods, the hydroponics mechanism is found to be the most popular mechanism in vertical farming across the globe. The hydroponic growing process requires approximately 10 per cent of the amount of water used in traditional methods. Simultaneously, building-based vertical farms are believed to generate better per square foot revenue than shipping container-based vertical farms, as the former uses lesser capital and incurs lower operating expenses (for the same area).

According to a spokesperson from Aerofarm, the global leader in vertical farming, 'The growing interest from the investment community will help accelerate the overall commercial expansion, R&D and boost the food supply chain challenges.'[9] The company claims to use 95 per cent less water, says it is 390 times more land efficient and grows thirty crops per season. Each plant is monitored on more than 1,30,000 data points that are reviewed and tested using predictive analytics to improve their growing systems. With remote monitoring and controls, it has minimized the typical risks associated with traditional agriculture.[10]

The market for vertical farming, however, is still emerging and moving towards attaining a mature state with multiple big and small players competing in the market. It is projected to reach US$9.73 billion by 2026, registering a CAGR of 25 per cent between 2021 and 2026.

These next-generation farming methods play a vital role in reducing the environmental impact of agriculture. Indoor farming also cuts down on the distance travelled in the supply chain and has gained prominence with increasing consumer interest in local products. With the shrinking agricultural land and resources coupled with the rising demand for organic produces, these environment-friendly and technologically advanced farming techniques have been gaining rapid popularity in recent years.

## Agricultural Biotechnology

The global agrigenomics market is majorly fuelled by rapid advances in the functional genomics sector with the adaptation of massive parallel sequencing technologies and the development of protocols to efficiently analyse cellular behaviour at the molecular level. For applied genomics in agriculture, molecular marker-assisted crop breeding has proved effective over conventional breeding programmes, with regard to the increasing scope, speed and efficiency of crop selection. Advanced genome characterization techniques have shown increased quality and yield of crops while at the same time requiring less fertilizers, pesticides and water. For livestock, the novel technologies are known to have greatly improvised the desirable traits, such as milk yield, meat quality and reproductive life.

DNA extraction can be used to modify plants by isolating DNA from organisms with desirable traits, such as resistance to pesticides, and injecting them into the genome of the plant. In the past, the process of extraction and purification of nucleic acids used to be complicated, time-consuming, labour-intensive and limited in terms of overall throughput.

Currently, there are many specialized methods that can be used to extract pure biomolecules, such as solution-based and column-based protocols. The manual method has come a long way over time, with various commercial offerings that include complete kits containing most components needed to isolate nucleic acid. However, most of them require repeated centrifugation steps, followed by the removal of supernatants depending on the type of specimen and additional mechanical treatment.

In agriculture, the associations between genes and resulting traits revealed by high-throughput approaches such as transcription profiling could be used to select more environmentally friendly chemicals for plant protection and develop plants with increased grain yields and better nutrition value, with more resistance to diseases and tolerance to abiotic stress. However, one of the major challenges to applying such approaches is the limited genomic information for most of the much-diversified crop species.

Beyond food and nutritional security, tools and techniques of genome analysis can also assist in detecting food safety issues such as spoilage and contamination, adulteration and economic fraud, as well as assisting traceability over the entire supply chain from farm to fork.

New breeding techniques based on applied genetics have revolutionized breeding strategies for crops and livestock by providing unprecedented access to genomic information. Genomics has also successfully furnished information about the biological status of important resources such as fisheries, crops and livestock health.

## Tech-Enhanced Kitchens: Smart Kitchens

Kitchens are the new laboratories in the era of the fourth industrial revolution or Industry 4.0. With the increasing mechanization of the kitchen, there is a device or appliance for nearly every activity in the cooking space. Emerging new technologies are now bringing deep changes in the way food is prepared, stored and disposed.

## 3D Printing in Food

3D printing in food is gaining special prominence across the world. The US Space agency NASA has promoted concepts like 3D-printed pizzas for astronauts and in recent years several startups have brought ground-breaking solutions with additive manufacturing technology.

Even in emerging markets like India, such technologies are gaining traction with welcome support from the government. Thanjavur-based Indian Institute of Food Processing Technology (IIFPT) is working on 3D printers to make food and also ways to convert agricultural waste into useful products.

With the new law by Parliament, IIFPT and the National Institute of Food Technology Entrepreneurship and Management at Kundli, near Delhi, have now become institutions of national importance and will be soon known as the National Institutes of Food Technology, Entrepreneurship and Management.[11] This critical move will provide functional autonomy to the institutes for launching relevant courses and research in food technology. Their mandate will also be to work with farmers to address issues such as food wastage. Using emerging technologies, agri-waste such as paddy husk or crop stubble is now being converted into sustainable packaging materials, while food wastes in restaurants are being treated, blended and 3D-printed into purees that can form base ingredients for baking.

The rise in demand for 3D printing can be attributed to the critical need for the reduction of wastage in the food sector and also to meet the evolving consumer preferences for specialized food products.

In addition to delighting customers with attractive and bespoke cuisine, 3D food printers are also steadily gaining importance in the healthcare segment. Hospitals can now install 3D food printers to create precision food and customized dishes for patients. As many patients need specific types of food based on their condition and the treatment they are undergoing, the healthcare service companies and elder-care homes can custom-produce food for their patients and maintain high nutritional levels.

## Robotics

For urban dwellers who want to consume food untouched by human hands, robotic kitchens are posing to be a great initiative. With time these robots are expected to become as indispensable to homeowners as washing machines and ovens. One such example is Britain's Moley Robotic Kitchen. 'The Moley Kitchen uses a combination of sensors and optical cameras to map ingredients, cookware and utensils within the kitchen. Subtle markers on handles and pan lids help robots to orientate the stainless-steel pots, pans and utensils. The robot's optical system can even spot dropped food and clean it up before and after cooking. An integrated UV lamp ensures the cooking area is kept germ free,' says the company.

Several startups in India have also invested in food tech solutions for domestic needs. Chennai-based RoboChef has been getting attention while others are making intelligent versions of dosa-making and roti-making machines. Be ready to work with robots in the kitchen soon.

## A Sprinkling of Artificial Intelligence Flavours

Wasabi KitKat, dosa-flavoured burger, green tea cookies or Mumbai Chowpatty seasoning—such flavours may appear unusual but point to a rising trend of creativity in taste. And much of this is being powered by AI-based technology. Food, flavours and aroma make for a memorable culinary experience. The skills of chefs and amateurs are often measured by their ability to bring disparate food products to meld together for a uniquely satisfying combination.

Such human ingenuity is being complemented by AI and other food tech solutions, which are coming up with new experiments to pander to our country-specific palates.

IBM's AI platform, Watson, for instance, has published a cookbook. Watson has collaborated with food giant McCormick to use AI to create fresh flavours. McCormick owns various brands including Kohinoor Rice and French's. 'Product developers across its global workforce are now able to explore flavour territories more quickly and efficiently, using AI to learn and predict new flavour combinations from hundreds of millions of data points across the areas of sensory science, consumer preference and flavour palates,' says McCormick. 'We co-create custom flavours for ten of the top ten food and beverage companies, and all top ten food service restaurant chains worldwide.'

Much of this also allows mass customization for consumers based on age and geography. Food science research firm Spoonshot has been helping companies develop data-science-based consumer insights. Working out of Bangalore and Minnesota, Spoonshot identifies future trends for food preferences. In January 2021 , the company launched a free version of its AI-based food pairing tool. The company processes 'data relating to the physical and chemical properties of ingredients and understand[s] how ingredient interactions impact a final recipe.'

Another firm Gastrograph AI has also been impressing the food world with the use of 'the first artificial intelligence platform to interpret and predict flavour preferences for over a billion unique consumer groups.' In focus groups with consumers, Gastrograph AI asks them to identify the flavours of specific products using a smartphone app. Consumers can try a new product and then identify various flavours on a digital map. These include floral, earthy, astringent, sour tastes among others. By tweaking various flavours over several sessions with focus groups, it can arrive at an ideal combination for new products being created by food companies. Not just flavours, Gastrograph AI also maps the consumers' own socio-economic profile, preferences, demographics, habits and locality. Such data can help create different flavour varieties of the same product for different markets.

Consumers just need to take a glance at their digital food apps or shop stores to witness the variety on offer. Using AI to create such a choice is often cheaper and allows companies to create new variants in a shorter time span. Consumers spoilt for choice and eager to experience new flavours are being pampered by AI algorithms.

## Plant-Based Meats and Alternatives

In recent times, with growing awareness of health and wellness, consumer preferences are notably shifting towards plant-based and organic food. Plant-based meat products are significantly replacing conventionally processed meat products, such as burgers, sausages and nuggets. They contain lower levels of saturated fat, cholesterol and calories than animal-based meat, and often have higher levels of micronutrients, such as zinc, iron and calcium.

The nutritional benefits of plant-based meats and their safety compared with conventional meat are some of the important factors contributing to gaining the attention of consumers.

The global plant-based meat market was valued at US$1.6 billion in 2020. It is projected to grow at a significant CAGR of 16.9 per cent during the forecasted period. The US accounted for the largest share of the North American market and was valued at US$1.35 billion in 2020.

In this sector, burger patties have been the largest and fastest growing plant-based meat product, growing at a CAGR of approximately 16.4 per cent during 2021–26.

In the dairy alternative sector, in terms of regions, the Asia–Pacific market accounted for the largest share of 47 per cent in 2020. The dairy alternatives market in the region is driven by large economies such as China, Japan and Australia, and a strong agricultural production base for plant-based sources. Europe is expected to be the fastest growing region in the global dairy alternatives market. European countries have shown tremendous growth potential due to the growing vegan population in the region. The global dairy alternatives market is projected to account for US 40.6 billion in 2026, growing at a CAGR of 10.3 per cent during the forecast period.

## Smart Logistics, Food Storage and Transportation

Consumer preferences for the food they consume have seen dramatic shifts and transformations in the last few years. Consumers are now more knowledgeable, aware and conscious, and prefer more locally grown organic food. Food that has travelled less to reach the kitchen or plate hence has less preservatives and chemicals. Storage and transportation are the other areas that have been crucial for the industry.

The unique requirements of storage, stock keeping unit (SKU) and transportation for food and beverages are benefiting substantially from digital innovations.

Blockchain is poised to greatly improve the performance of supply chains, especially the new permissioned blockchains where participation is restricted to known supply chain partners, data standards and governance rules. With the implementation of laws and regulations such as the Food Safety Modernization Act (2011) and the Drug Supply Chain Security Act (2013) in the United States and the Falsified Medicines Directive (2013) and the European Green Deal in Europe, companies are now required to trace the movement of their products, maintain records and show proof of identity. They can also measure the environmental impact of such activities along the supply chain.[12] Hence, collecting and analysing data would play a crucial role in achieving the goals. The IoT facilitates data collection from different stages of a supply chain, which is further recorded and aligned for predictive analytics. For example, Ripe.io, an agri-tech organization, used traceability data from tomato production to relate the flavour of ripened tomatoes to growing conditions. Predictive analytics enabled the firm to grow different types of tomatoes according to the needs of different customer segments.

In addition to these, key factors such as maintaining quality, regulatory restrictions, seasonal changes, hygiene standards, low shelf life and higher scale of production are all getting streamlined with digitization. Tech-powered warehouses can not only ensure reduction in operational/labour costs but also facilitate higher density storage, safer work environment, faster goods-to-person picking times and faster order fulfilment. According to Jeff Beck, CEO at Soft Robotics, the technology leaders in food and beverages, consumer packaged goods and logistics, 'the vulnerabilities of the food supply chain have been illuminated by the pandemic making it clear that automation/ digitization has graduated from a nice-to-have to a must-have across all large-scale food production operations.'[13]

Warehouse management to create already been remodelling the warehouse space. Hybrid semiautomated warehousing systems are gaining momentum.[14] It is a set-up that utilizes both automation solutions and labour in key areas to improve warehouse performance. Manufacturers are also incorporating technology solutions such as order-picking technologies (for example, pick-to-light technology, voice technology, sortation systems), barcoding, radio frequency identification (RFID) and automated storage and retrieval systems (ASRS) to achieve a sustainable warehousing system.[15] The adoption of ASRS is expected to expand at a pace of over 9.1 per cent on an annual basis, mostly due to its application in retail warehouses.[16] Also, automated guided vehicles (AGVs) undertake a series of tasks from unloading and loading trucks to transporting large items across warehouse floors. These operations can be performed in harsh conditions such as freezers and cold storage environments for longer periods.

Technology in supply chain has made traceability and transparency possible, which is in line with food safety protocols and keeps sustainability and energy efficiency at the core of every operation. Technologies such as edge computing, blockchain, robotics and cybersecurity are bringing holistic changes in the way food and beverages companies operate.

## Industry Outlook

In addition to the environmental aspect, the major constraint faced by the food and beverages sector is labour shortage. The issue has been further intensified by the COVID-19 pandemic with prolonged lockdowns and complete shutdowns. According to the farmer's association CIA,[17] Malaysia, the world's second-largest palm oil producer, lost about 30 per cent of the potential output of edible oil due to the dearth of workers. Shrimp production in southern Vietnam—one of the world's top exporters—dropped by 60 per cent to 70 per cent from before the pandemic. And a fifth of tomato production in the south of Italy was lost in 2021, due to transport paralysis.

Even with the sector ramping up technologies such as robotics, ML, data science, blockchain, automation and AI, the impact of labour shortage has been particularly intense as the rate of tech adoption is still considered low compared to other industries. But now the industry has shifted focus and is working aggressively to adopt automation and AI to address labour shortage issues. A report by *The New York Times* highlighted how the grocery industry is leaning more on technology to free up employees for higher skilled occupations and to deal with the huge demand during the pandemic.[18] In the article, a representative from Brain Corp, a software designing organization for automated floor cleaners, said that autonomous floor care robot usage has risen to about 8,000 hours of daily work—a 13 per cent increase from pre-pandemic use. This allows workers to engage in more productive activities.

According to an analysis by McKinsey and Company,[19] nearly three quarters of food service and accommodation tasks could be automated. Industrial robots are working along with AI, thermal scanners and lasers to chop vegetables, grill hamburgers or prepare other foods or perform similar tasks. The AI is also being deployed into cooking processes, optimizing recipes and ingredients selection, while chef robots are now real. At the front-end of restaurants, there are automated services where voice- or facial recognition-activated cashiers could take orders and payments or assign tables.

Other prominent changes include the rise of contactless solutions based on AI and digital payments, the need for 'at home' experiences and cloud kitchens.

## Digital Innovations for a Food Secure Nation

The UAE set into motion a number of initiatives and policies to make it the most food-secure nation as part of its National Food Security Strategy 2051.[20] To achieve this vision, the UAE has been steadily investing in new agri-tech, sustainable agriculture practices, and offering support and subsidies to farmers and producers to make them more self-reliant. This strategy will also help to provide new jobs and raise US$6 billion for the country's economy. The UAE's food trade already exceeds AED100 billion annually, making the country a global food logistics hub. The UNDP Accelerator Lab India is leading a network of partners for reimagining Indian food systems while addressing various

challenges through its many agri-tech initiatives.[21] The lab also
plans to scale up its blockchain platform jointly with Spices Board
India to cover major spice varieties and spice-growing regions in
India. It has initiated Data for Policy in partnership with the
Telangana government, the Rockefeller Foundation and several
other stakeholders to strengthen climate resilience in agriculture
programmes and policies. The initiative leverages open-source
technologies and digital public good platforms to engage citizen
scientists to generate data insights on climate resilience.

## Summary

The fundamentals of growing food will not change in the near
future. Nature will continue to take care of that. However, the
application of science and technology will ensure that agro-
produce yields more and delivers faster. Sustainable processes
will help to reduce the burden on earth while trying to feed the
growing billions. The lack of arable land and water in an era
of climate change can only be mitigated by the smarter use of
science and technology.

# 3

# The Chemistry of Chemicals

M etals are tough and solid. They are reliable as they stay fixed in the shape or form in which they are created. The new version of metals has a different personality though, and is shape-shifting. As per a note by Massachusetts Institute of Technology, 'The discovery of a new category of shape-memory materials made of ceramic rather than of metal could open up a new range of applications, especially for high-temperature settings, such as actuators inside a jet engine or a deep borehole.' The new findings were reported in the journal *Nature*, in a paper by former doctoral student Edward Pang PhD '21 and professors Gregory Olson and Christopher Schuh, all in MIT's department of materials science and engineering. 'One common application of shape-memory materials is relief valves, where if a tank of something exceeds a certain critical temperature, the valve is triggered by that heat, automatically opening to relieve pressure and prevent explosion. The new ceramic material could now extend that capability to far higher-temperature situations than present materials could handle.'[1]

Several such discoveries and inventions are changing the world around us.

We can call them magic molecules. The chemistry that creates surfaces, food and products is changing life at a nano level for all of us. From low-cost efficiencies to sustainability to making lightweight products, chemical science is at the core of most innovation and disruption.

The evolving consumer preferences (and consciousness) towards environment-friendly products and solutions has intensified the chemical industry to focus on aspects such as sustainability, demographics and technology.[2] According to a Deloitte report, 'A large number of chemical companies are expected to increase investment in their R&D capabilities. They have begun to leverage advances in decarbonization and recycling technologies to lower their and their customers' carbon footprint, and also reduce plastic waste.' The report adds that 2022 is expected to witness more industry players creating goals and plans around the abatement of emissions and monetization of waste.[3] The demand for 'new and sustainable chemical products' is expected to be much higher in the coming years and will require chemical companies to bring in fundamental changes coupled with the right technology-led innovations.

The industry is rapidly transforming itself and embracing green chemistry, smart chemicals and advanced materials. Environmental Protection Agency defines green chemistry as 'the design of chemical products and processes that reduce or eliminate the use or generation of hazardous substances'. Green chemistry is relevant across the life cycle of a product and is also known as sustainable chemistry. From design to manufacture, to use and final disposal, green chemistry is the good chemistry that aims to minimize the toll of a manufacturing process on the environment.[4]

## Sustainability in Chemicals

One example in this context is green jeans. The traditional method of manufacturing one pair of jeans requires over 2,500 gallons of water, approximately a pound of chemicals and large amounts of energy. Every year, over two billion jeans are produced worldwide. Green jeans, however, is the 'advanced denim'[5] where manufacturers can produce one pair of jeans using up to 92 per cent less water and up to 30 per cent less energy as compared to the conventional denim production process. This manufacturing method induces green chemistry for production.

As PreScouter technical director Marija Jovic notes, '"Green chemistry" is the foundation of a sustainable future and the way to be at the frontier of business and consumer needs.' The growth of the market is mainly driven by the growing popularity of bio-based packaging to combat the depleting reserves of fossil fuels across the world. Bio-based packaging materials are made from renewable and environment-friendly sources such as animal wastes and plants. They are also non-toxic, have low production costs, need less raw material for their production and can be disposed of easily. This, in turn, helps in reducing the overall carbon footprint.

Major segments driving the growth for green chemistry include—one, the beauty products and personal care category, resulting from rising awareness of the benefits of bio-based personal hygiene and beauty products over synthetic chemical-based beauty products and two, the food and beverages category resulting from the growing requirement for food additives made from natural ingredients such as organic acids like lactic acid, which are acids highly used for preserving food items.[6]

Sustainable chemicals are further boosted by the ongoing digital transformations across industries. Digital technologies extend powerful tools to respond to and facilitate smoother transitions and higher efficiencies in the industry. Tools such as AI, blockchain, the industrial internet of things (IIoT), data analytics and cloud are already inducing paradigm shifts to attain manufacturing efficiencies and sustainability. According to a World Economic Forum report, digitalization in the chemical and advanced manufacturing industry has the potential to reduce $CO_2$ emissions by 60–100 million tonnes and save lives and avoid over 2,000 injuries over the next decade.[7] For example, AkzoNobel's big data service Intertrac Vision has helped shipping firms save fuel and cut emissions dramatically. It analyses over 3.5 billion data points to decide the right coatings for a specific ship. These coatings promote a reduction in biofouling (the accumulation of micro-organisms, plants and algae on a ship's hull) and thereby reduce drag and boost fuel efficiency.[8]

From a demographic aspect, chemistry and advanced materials companies need to adapt to shifts occurring in the industry's workforce. Organizations in developed markets, such as Japan, Europe and North America, are facing a challenge of an aging workforce. They are at risk of losing vital knowledge and insights with a high retiring population. It has also become increasingly important to ensure integrated and real-time sharing of knowledge across businesses, due to the extensive adoption of mobile and cloud solutions. As a result, the need to transfer valuable industry skills and knowledge quickly and effectively to younger colleagues is now ever more critical.

The chemical industry is at a juncture where it needs to capture the opportunities to upskill people on a war footing.[9] The sector needs to redefine its entire value chains and business models to adapt to the current trends of the digital and circular economy.

## Chemistry 4.0

Today, the chemistry and advanced materials sector is one of the key enablers of the fourth industrial revolution or Industry 4.0 as well as the digital revolution. Electrical vehicles, drones, smartphones, high-speed internet and a range of other sectoral innovations require massive support from this sector. The contributions facilitate other sectors and turn ideas into advanced products and unique innovations. Some of the examples include the use of chlorosilanes in cables to deliver fibreoptic properties needed for fast, trouble-free data transfer, use of plastics, composites and batteries for electric vehicles and drones and use of the substrate, backplane and transparent conductors for smartphones and tablets.[10]

This sector itself is witnessing massive digital transformations across its value chain. It is the amalgamation of multiple technologies that is creating value for this sector and the society at large. Today, a digitally bolstered track-and-trace solution (such as blockchain technology for information security) empowers companies to exchange information efficiently and safely throughout their product's life cycle. Firms are able to aggregate information about the origin, journey, composition and carbon footprint of a material or product along the supply chain. This eases regulatory compliance and recycling efforts and helps meet the demand from consumers for traceability and transparency of products and materials. Buyers want to know about quality and genuineness. A blockchain-based system can track the product from its origin to its manufacture.

Senior executives of the chemistry and advanced materials sector strongly believe in the transformational effect of digitalization on their industry. But most are yet to adapt to change. 'Only a handful of companies are taking on the disruptive forces, making dynamic decisions and successfully remaking industries,' an Accenture report says.

Its research shows that by 2025, digitization could unlock up to $550 billion of value for the chemical industry. The champions in the chemical industry 'understand that digital technology is creating more discerning customers who want connected products that don't pollute, save time, and are easy to use.'[11]

As chemistry and advanced materials companies adapt to the circular economy concepts, these are often driven by product-related innovation, such as bio-based plastics.

Digitalization is accelerating the circular economy initiatives, within sector boundaries as well as along the value chain. The entire chemical industry is witnessing a move towards increased automation for cost optimization and addressing the growing skills shortage. These technologies offer higher levels of connectivity and speed to access, process and analyse massive databases. Mobility, cloud, in-memory computing, IoT, machine learning and blockchain are acting as game changers in the chemical industry. They are the enablers of green chemistry to turn it into a reality that is poised to play an important role in making products that are safe for humans and for the environment. As per a MarketsandMarkets report on IoT in the chemical industry referring to International Federation of Robotics data, the annual sales volume has increased by 114 per cent over 2013−17.

During  021, this volume grew by 13.5 per cent to 4,35,000 units of annual installation.

## Startups and Innovation

The new entrants in the industry are further intensifying the transformation and disruption along the value chain. For instance, Biotech startups Zymergen and Synthace are using digital technology to enhance their R&D and have digitized their research procedure with machine learning and robotics. Another example is 3D printing. By fully integrating 3D-printing software, hardware and advanced materials, the new entrants are able to provide customized services that give more than just granulate and additives, which the traditional organizations still need to catch up with.

A large number of startups are working on a variety of solutions and promising bio-based and sustainable chemicals. From bio-plastics, plant-based surfactants that are used for manufacturing detergents, to natural fibres and environment-friendly materials, startups are working on a series of bio-based alternatives. The solutions generally utilize waste biomass and do not impact food or feed supplies. A few examples of these innovations are as follows.

A French startups called Evertree is developing sustainable alternatives to fossil fuel-based industrial chemicals. It produces adhesive solutions that are bio-sourced instead of petro-sourced resins. Its product Green Ultimate uses 60 per cent less fossil carbon to manufacture than a urea-formaldehyde resin. The rapeseed and sunflower seeds used for the solution are sourced locally to reduce the impact of transport and, hence, lower the carbon footprint.

CH-Bioforce is a Finnish startup that develops biomass fractionation technology, a process claimed to be almost chemical-free. The startup's process uses pressurized hot water extraction (PHWE) to get valuable bio-based chemicals from wood and straw. Recently, CH-Bioforce was reported to be helping the world's biggest brewing company, AB InBev, turn brewing waste into textiles.[12]

The US-based startup Sironix Renewables provides plant-based surfactants that are used for application in detergents, agriculture and oil recovery. The organization uses non-competitive plant sources, such as soy and algal oil, to synthesize surfactants that ensure the elimination of toxic byproducts. The manufacturing industry then uses these surfactants to develop detergents that further reduce the environmental footprint of their operations.

## Paints and Coatings

Paint and coatings can be a liquid or powder mixture that converts into solid film after application to a surface in a thin layer. A coating is a covering that is applied to a surface for decoration and protection. It includes all organic and inorganic coatings: enamels, varnishes, emulsions and bituminous coatings. Coating is used broadly to refer to any coloured or clear product, and paint is used to describe a pigmented product with an organic or inorganic binder.

The market size of paints and coatings is projected to grow from US$184.0 billion in 2021 to US$212.3 billion by 2026, at a CAGR of 2.9 per cent during the forecast period. The rapid growth in the housing and construction sector, increasing gross domestic product (GDP), growing urbanization and increasing disposable income are driving the paints and coatings market. Technological advancements in end-use industries such as automotive, marine, aerospace, wood and other industries are also supporting the growth.

The construction industry's demand for environment-friendly and healthier coating systems and the rising need to improve performance, durability and aesthetics are the key factors contributing to the growth of the paints and coatings market. Paints and coatings are widely used because of their durability, appearance, quality and eco-friendly anti-microbial properties. Asia–Pacific is the biggest market, and the per capita consumption in the region is rising significantly.

The increasing demand for environment-friendly characteristics has been one of the most important trends observed in the coatings industry in the last ten years, largely influenced by the stringent European Union regulations regarding the reduction of volatile organic compound (VOC) emissions in the coating life cycle. Most of these regulations state the VOC limits for various types of paints that need to be strictly followed. These regulations also require the product package to carry an indication of the VOC content and limit. With the growing awareness regarding the harmful effects of VOC emissions supported by regulations, there has been a gradual shift in demand from solvent-borne coatings to environment-friendly products, such as waterborne, powder coatings, high solids and UV-curable coatings, as these products contain fewer solvents that evaporate during the curing phase. Powder coatings have gained substantial popularity, as they release negligible VOCs, if any, into the atmosphere and contain no solvents.

Waterborne coatings account for the largest market share in the paints and coatings market. They are used widely in many end-use industries, such as automotive, furniture, rail coatings, electrical and electronics, energy and general industries.

Advancements in powder coatings technology, thin-film powders (one mil or thinner), UV-cured powders, lower temperature cure powders and powders that are resistant to high heat clear coats are driving the market. For more than thirty years, powder coatings have revolutionized the finishing industry by providing a superior, durable and environment-friendly finish, particularly for metal products, such as appliances, automotive parts, sporting goods and other commercial and industrial products.

Technological advancements in powder coatings materials, their unique applications and advanced curing methods have enhanced the use of powder coatings in heat-sensitive substrates. Medium-density fibreboard (MDF), a combination of panel-bonding synthetic resin with particles of wood, is one of the most important advancements in powder coatings. MDF is suitable for powder coating applications owing to its low porosity and homogeneous surface. Powder coatings are increasingly used on MDF products for finishing. The MDF products include doors, kitchen and bath cabinets, office furniture, store fixtures and displays and ready-to-assemble furniture for offices and homes.

As the chemical industry is a significant direct emitter of $CO_2$, leading sectors have started to incorporate carbon and broader environmental targets into their agendas. The need for green coatings was created by the consistent shift towards reducing VOCs in decorative paint. The VOC laws are consistently evolving at global and regional levels. Also, green building programmes such as LEED are pushing the demand for green coatings. There is a strong demand for it across all segments, with interior applications driving the demand the most.[13]

## Biodegradable Plastics

Plastics are another big challenge as a pollutant in our ecosystem, especially single-use plastics. Going by projections, 2050 will see more plastics than fish in the oceans. Hence, the industry is focusing on compostable, biodegradable, oxo-degradable or bio-based plastics as a solution to this challenge. Biodegradable plastics break down 60 per cent and more within 180 days or less, as opposed to traditional plastics, which take around 1,000 years to break down.

The global biodegradable plastics market size is set to grow from US$7.7 billion in 2021 to US$23.3 billion by 2026, at a CAGR of 24.9 per cent. The growth is driven by end-use segments, stringent regulatory and sustainability mandates, along with growing concerns for the environment.

## Sustainable Adhesives

The growing population and higher living standards have pushed the demand for adhesives and, subsequently the need for environment-friendly solutions. Sustainable adhesives generally belong to one of three groups: solventless adhesives, waterborne adhesives and bio-based adhesives.[14] New forms of renewable adhesives include those made of beeswax and plant, recyclable adhesives, biodegradable and compostable green adhesives and repulpable adhesives.

The Accenture 2020 Global Buyer Values Study for Chemicals found that customers are willing to buy more and pay more if their needs are met.[15] Moreover, a recent McKinsey survey of the European chemical industry showed that 55 per cent of buyers of petrochemical products are keen to adopt digital channels that can provide efficiency and add value. In the case of specialty chemicals, the share is even higher with 82 per cent of customers willing to adopt digital platforms.[16]

## Adhesive Tapes

Adhesive tape consists of a narrow flexible carrier or backing material, typically used to hold or fasten a substrate. At room temperature, it adheres to a variety of surfaces with the placement of light (finger) pressure without any change in phase (liquid to solid). The demand for adhesive tapes has increased in the healthcare, electrical and electronics and automotive industries. In the healthcare industry, adhesive tapes are applied to surgical containers, monitoring electrodes and other medical devices. Currently, these tapes are used for covering wounds, fixing cover shields during surgeries and in antiseptic rooms, for cleaning purposes. In the electrical and electronics industry, a wide range of adhesive tapes is used for special applications in the manufacturing and assembly of electronic components. In the automotive industry, these are used for attaching components onto the outer surfaces of car bodies and for a variety of functions in the interiors of automobiles.

The global adhesive tape market size was US$59.2 billion in 2020 and is projected to reach US$83.8 billion by 2026, at a CAGR of 5.8 per cent between 2021 and 2026.

In the electrical and electronics industry, the trend towards using lightweight devices is leading to the increasing application of adhesive tapes.

## The Lightweighting Market

The material market is seeing a huge disruption. Lightweight material has gained its foothold in multiple industries ranging from aerospace to the sporting goods industry. Composites have emerged as the winner among all lightweighting materials such as aluminium alloys, high-strength steels, electric vehicles, FCVs, NGVs and hydrogen tanks.

A composite is a mixture of two materials with different properties, such as mechanical, micro-cracking and fatigue resistance, remarkable tensile strength, electrical conductivity and high strength-to-weight ratio, which, when combined, offers an end product with superior properties.

The composites market is expected to witness significant growth during this decade. This growth will be mainly attributed to its increasing application in the automotive, aerospace and defence, construction and other end-use industries. Tax incentives and low crude oil prices are further pushing the growth of the composites market.

The capability of composites to maintain a greater strength-to-weight ratio allows more efficient structural and aerodynamic designs. There has been a paradigm shift in aircraft design at Boeing and Airbus, with aerospace composites considered primary structures. All wide-body aeroplanes designed by both manufacturers are now based on the new paradigm. As per MarketsandMarkets research, in the new aircraft programmes of Boeing and Airbus, such as the 787 Dreamliner, 777X and A350XWB groups, composites comprise 50 per cent of all materials used in the aircraft. The extensive usage of these advanced aircraft is attributed to higher fatigue tolerance, which helps in improving or increasing the structural components, such as bigger passenger windows and a lower cabin altitude on cruises than conventional jetliners. Both Boeing and Airbus are projecting multibillion-dollar markets for new aeroplanes over the next twenty years, particularly in Asia–Pacific, which would subsequently drive the composites market.

Car manufacturers are using new lightweight materials for manufacturing their products. Composites are the best substitute for traditional heavy materials such as steel and aluminium to fabricate a car body. They are largely used in making the chassis, door panels, monocoque, interior and door panels, and other car body parts. When used in car body fabrication, they provide a 25 per cent to 70 per cent weight reduction compared to the traditional materials, which improves mileage as well as the strength-to-weight ratio of a car, making it stiff against accidents, thus providing a high level of safety to the passengers.

The luxury car segment has witnessed rapid growth, which is significantly driving the demand for high-strength aluminium alloys. Manufacturers prefer adopting lightweight alloys to improve the vehicle's performance.

Natural fibre composites are disrupting the lightweighting material market. It is emerging as an alternative to glass fibre composites in many end-use industries, such as automotive parts, building structures and consumer goods. Natural fibre reinforcements are mostly used in interior applications of vehicles and are widely used in automotive applications as they are renewable resources and have lower environmental footprints than carbon or glass fibres. This can help automotive equipment manufacturers meet stringent regulations.

According to MarketsandMarkets estimates, the global lightweighting material market size was US$90 billion in 2021 and is expected to reach US$130 billion by 2026 at a CAGR of 7.6 per cent from 2021 to 2026.

Composites are the leading lightweighting material market. The composites market size was US$76.2 billion in 2020 and is projected to reach US$126.4 billion by 2026. It is projected to register a CAGR of 7.5 per cent between 2021 and 2026, owing to the high demand from various end-use industries worldwide.

## 3D Printing and Materials

3D printing has been regarded as one of the major disruptive technologies of this century, transitioning from prototyping to a potential production method, also referred to as additive manufacturing. It is expected to have a positive impact on various end-use industries, such as aerospace and defence, healthcare, automotive and consumer goods, owing to the mass customization offered by this process.

The process entails building an object, layer by layer, with the use of a thin material from a 3D digital model.

Plastics and metals are mainly used to create complex objects. High-performance plastic has emerged as a key material in the 3D printing material market and the aircraft industry is one of the early adopters. This material is highly useful for producing complex and intricate parts as it can withstand extreme temperature conditions. Aircraft and auto manufacturers are using the 3D printing process to integrate high-performance thermoplastics into their manufacturing. 'Manufacturers across the aerospace industry are unified in their goal of optimal strength-to-weight ratios—as the lighter the aircraft, the more fuel efficient. For this reason, thermoplastics and other polymer materials have made a tremendously positive impact in the global industry,' says CDI Energy Products, a Michelin Group material science company.[17]

According to GE, 'The 3D printing of both jet engine prototypes and end-use parts is already having a significant impact on development and production.' According to the company, the next-generation GE9X from GE Aviation will use nineteen 3D-printed fuel nozzles to help power the next generation of wide-body aircraft like the Boeing 777X. The GE9X is the largest and most powerful jet engine ever manufactured—the front fan alone measures 11 feet in diameter. While it is approximately 10 per cent more fuel-efficient than its predecessor, it still generates 100,000 pounds of thrust at takeoff.[18]

Polyetheretherketone (PEEK) has a high demand from the medical 3D printing industry. It offers a continuous rating service above 240°Celsius and maintains its stiffness up to 170°Celsius, which means this 3D printing high-performance plastic can be autoclaved, which is necessary for many applications in the biomedical field. Further, this material is biocompatible and certified for use in implants—PEEK has a very high demand for bone and spine implants.

Bioceramics such as hydroxyapatite and tricalcium phosphate have also disrupted the material market in the medical and healthcare 3D printing market. The healthcare industry is more inclined to use bioceramic material for 3D printing of custom-bone implants as they are non-reactive to body cells, unlike their metal counterparts. These materials are resorbable by the body and help in reconstructing the natural bone of the patient.

Similarly, zirconium is widely used for oral implants as it gives a similar look to the original teeth and the added advantage of customization. Therefore, there is a rise in partnerships of dental professionals with 3D printing solution providers.

Mass customization is the current revolution in the 3D printing industry, which has made life easier as consumers can create designs and develop new paradigms by crafting various designs on the computer and printing them. For plastic objects, the printers can be located at retail stores, and for metal and other materials, it can be placed at specialized offsite facilities. In either case, the final product cost will be affordable for customers. Mass customization enabled by 3D printing has led to an increased demand for different 3D printing materials.

3D-printed consumer goods are expected to propel the growth of the 3D printing materials market in the near future. Complex and customized designs can be achieved—jewellers, watchmakers and other gadget companies are highly inclined towards mass customization to cater to specific requirements.

According to MarketsandMarkets estimates, the global 3D printing material market size was US$1.6 billion in 2020 and is expected to reach US$4.5 billion by 2025 at a CAGR of 23.5 per cent from 2020 to 2025.

In 3D printing, the choice of material is based on the printer used. In terms of the demand, plastic materials account for a major share, followed by metals. Plastics are mainly used in the form of a filament, whereas metals are generally used in powder form.

The metal 3D printing material segment holds a majority of the share in the 3D printing materials market in terms of volume. Plastic 3D printing material accounted for US$869 million in 2020. This high consumption is primarily attributed to the growing usage in the automotive and aerospace end-use industry, and it is thus expected to be the fastest growing segment.

The high cost of 3D printing materials has been a significant point of concern associated with its market growth. A number of applications for 3D printing materials have been discovered but they face many restrictions due to the high costs. Developing low-cost technologies for manufacturing 3D printing materials is a major challenge for all researchers and key manufacturers.

One of the key challenges is to reduce the lead time associated with these materials, especially metals, which need a substantial period to be made into the end product. Manufacturers need to work on existing materials and technologies catering to the 3D printing industry as the high lead time restricts switching to additive manufacturing from the conventional manufacturing process, which is hampering the adoption of 3D printing in major end-use industries.

## Summary

There is magic at the molecular level, which we benefit from but do not often realize. Chemicals and materials that improve the nuts and bolts of technical systems have awe-inducing abilities. An average consumer or business leader may not understand the world of polymers and resin or bio-lubricants and composites. But these are quietly transforming the underpinnings of nearly every sector. It is time to take a closer look at the molecules that influence our world.

# 4

# Smart Manufacturing Advances Further

The sight of a metallic, human-like walking machine is common in movies. It is not so common in real life. Companies across the world though are continuing to invest in and create increasingly human robots. The high-decibel launch of a biped robot Optimus by Tesla sparked the question of who needs walking robots. The answer is simple. The smart manufacturing world needs them more than ever.

For most of us, a machine that moves around on its own doing work is a normal sight—a mop machine moving around at an airport terminal, a boxy robot holding a tray in a restaurant or a cylindrical robot delivering medicines inside a hospital. Robotic and automated machines on wheels have become fairly ubiquitous.

By themselves, the robot may not be a mass product right now but will be increasingly useful in sectors such as mining, energy, manufacturing and construction. And the technology used for its individual parts will be of great importance and utility.

The hands of Tesla Optimus are 'biologically inspired design'. This means that the various joints in the limbs and fingers are far more dexterous. If a robot's fingers are able to lift a coin or thread a needle, then such a skill can be deployed in precision manufacturing. While the robots may not walk, they will be able to think and decide to drive the future of manufacturing.

## Smart and Advanced Manufacturing

Smart manufacturing is no longer just about higher production at lower costs with the use of technology. When IoT and AI began to take hold of the manufacturing processes across sectors, the major benefits noted were a reduction in manufacturing time, better predictive maintenance, the possibility of remote repairs and enhanced visibility of the supply chain.

In the fifth industrial revolution's manufacturing processes, the goals of efficiency are being complemented by sustainable production objectives. Hence, for the renewed set of targets, emerging technologies continue to play a critical and enabling role.

A clutch of global companies is demonstrating the future of sustainable and smart manufacturing. The World Economic Forum (WEF) has set up the Global Lighthouse Network as a community of world-leading manufacturing facilities and value chains, which are using the fourth industrial revolution or Industry 4.0 technologies to improve efficiency along with environmental stewardship.

'By deploying advanced technologies such as robotics and AI in the production chain, more than half of all factories are making an impact on environmental sustainability through their Industry 4.0 transformations,' says a WEF report. Quoting an example, WEF says that a consumer healthcare company combined advanced controls with green technology to deploy a sensor-fed automated system to cut energy consumption. This resulted in 25 per cent less energy consumption and 18 per cent reduction in $CO_2$.

The Lighthouse Network includes more than ninety factories across the world from a diverse set of sectors, including pharmaceuticals, consumer products and various advanced technological products that are showing the way ahead for manufacturing. The WEF says that these factory sites are 'demonstrating how Industry 4.0 technologies can increase profit, with a positive impact on the environment'.

In March 2022, two such factories in India were included in the Lighthouse Network sites: Hindustan Unilever Limited (HUL) factory in Dapada near Mumbai and Schneider Electric's smart factory in Hyderabad. They have adopted technologies that can improve productivity while complying with green practices. The HUL factory emphasizes the impact on the environment as much as production efficiency. It produces about three million units per day for brands such as Surf Excel, Vim, Rin and Wheel. With machine learning and advanced analytics, water consumption and energy have been reduced by 31 per cent, while greenhouse gas emissions have lowered by 54 per cent.

Enabled by AI, deep learning, IIoT infrastructure, and both predictive and prescriptive analytics, these factories are minimizing manufacturing defect rates, non-quality costs and customer lead times, while simultaneously improving efficiency and sustainability. Companies such as HUL and Schneider Electric are leading the pack and playing a catalytic role in achieving a larger momentum for sustainability in production.

Another lighthouse example is from the factory of SVOLT Energy
Technology in Jiangsu province of China. Rockwell Automation
is helping SVOLT to enhance sustainable manufacturing of
lithium-ion and battery systems for electric vehicles and energy
storage.

Rockwell says it helped SVOLT identify priority areas to
transform manufacturing capabilities. It is helping SVOLT
implement changes through smart manufacturing and AI-driven
technologies.

When fully implemented, Rockwell will help SVOLT achieve
many goals, including 20 per cent reduction in manufacturing
costs; 20 per cent increase in per capita output and 67 per cent
reduction in ramp-up cycle.[1]

Industrial giants will have to work with their suppliers
to ensure that even small and medium manufacturers are
incentivized to use smart technologies for green objectives.

With sustainable production at its core, the smart manufacturing
market is growing rapidly with the adoption of Industry 4.0
principles across sectors such as oil and gas, food and beverages
and chemicals and automotive industries. Most processes and
systems in the manufacturing sector are now being automated,
which is allowing production units to operate 24×7 with zero
human errors. It helps decrease the total production cycle
time and maintain the quality of processes right from the raw
materials stage to the development of final products. With
automation solutions such as supervisory control and data
acquisition, human machine interface, distributed control
system, remote terminal unit, and programmable logic controller,
machines deployed in manufacturing plants can be operated

and controlled seamlessly with little or no human intervention. These technologies keep updating and evolving right from advanced to developing economies, and the upgrades ensure ease of integration with communication technologies such as 5G and infrastructure supporting IIoT to cutting-edge technologies such as edge computing in the industrial control environment.

According to MarketsandMarkets estimates, the global smart manufacturing market was valued at US$88.7 billion in 2021 and is projected to reach US$228.15 billion by 2027; it is expected to grow at a CAGR of 18.5 per cent from 2022 to 2027. In terms of the volume of industrial robots, the market registered a shipment of 3,51,000 units in 2020 and is expected to grow at a CAGR of 16.1 per cent to reach 8,17,000 units by 2026.

The major drivers of the smart manufacturing market include the growing adoption of industrial automation technologies, rising emphasis on its use in manufacturing processes, increasing government involvement in supporting it, growing emphasis on regulatory compliances, increasing complexities in the supply chain and surging demand for software systems that reduce time and cost.

According to a McKinsey survey of over 400 global manufacturing companies,[2] 94 per cent of the respondents indicated that Industry 4.0 helped them to keep their operations running during the pandemic, while 56 per cent said that the digital transformations they undertook were highly critical to their pandemic responses. Organizations that lagged in scaling their digital adoption had to take it as a serious wake-up call. They were forced to review their operational strategies and refocus on their Industry 4.0 capabilities.

The core of Industry 4.0 or smart manufacturing revolves around improving operational efficiency and mitigating losses by implementing innovative technologies that help in forecasting, transportation, logistics and predictive maintenance, inventory optimization, cycle time reduction or supply chain optimization. For example, Augury, one of the first unicorn technology companies in the global manufacturing sector, worked with Colgate-Palmolive and reportedly saved 2.8 million tubes of toothpaste. A leading biotech drug-maker and marketer Amgen set up an inspection system with AI. With the use of visual inspection to look at filled syringes, it was able to cut false rejects by 60 per cent.

In this chapter, we will provide an insight into some of the major technological innovations that are bringing ingenious transformations in the sector.

## Battery Technology

With surging demand for automation and battery-operated material-handling equipment, there has been an increased deployment of batteries in industries. A battery is an energy-storage device that is used extensively in transportation, consumer electronics, power and utility applications, and for industrial, commercial, residential and medical purposes. The currently available battery technology is based on materials used such as lead-acid batteries, lithium-ion batteries, nickel-metal hydride batteries and sodium-based batteries. However, several chemistries and innovative technologies are being developed to counter the limitations of available battery technology, including high cost, raw material sourcing problems and overheating.

Over the years, various advancements have taken place based on battery technology type. Today, battery technology can be classified into lithium-ion batteries; lead-acid batteries; nickel-metal hydride batteries and other battery technologies, which include alkaline battery, zinc-based battery, sodium-based battery and flow battery.

The battery technology market was valued at US$85.9 billion in 2019 and is projected to reach US$152.3 billion by 2025; it is expected to grow at a CAGR of 10.6 per cent from 2020 to 2025.

Lithium-ion and lead-acid batteries are among the highly adopted batteries in commercial, residential and utility applications. Lithium-ion batteries are one of the most efficient energy storage devices used worldwide. However, recent developments and claims made by the manufacturers and automobile companies suggest that the prices of these batteries are expected to decline substantially in the coming years.

According to MarketsandMarkets, the cost of lithium-ion batteries could decline to US$160 per kWh by 2025, which will fuel the adoption of these batteries across various applications. Other key factors propelling the battery technology market growth are the increasing use of electric and hybrid electric vehicles and the rising adoption in the renewable energy industry.

A metal-air battery is one of the most suitable candidates to meet the power storage demand. These batteries generally comprise a metal anode, an air cathode and an electrolyte. The metal at the anode in the battery gets oxidized to produce metal ions, which move through the electrolyte to the cathode and react with oxygen in the air to form metal oxides to produce energy.

The development of innovative designs of consumer electronics, including smartwatches and fitness bands, has generated the need for compact and flexible components such as different types of sensing and battery technologies to be deployed in these devices.

## Future of Wireless Charging

According to MarketsandMarkets, the development of Industry 4.0 is expected to boost the adoption of wireless charging in various end-user segments. Automatic wireless charging technology is used for mobile robots, drones and cordless tools and instruments, eliminating the complex docking mechanism process, and labour-intensive manual recharging and battery replacement.

Wireless charging technology eliminates the need to carry the USB-C charger. It allows the charging of multiple devices on the same charging pads and eliminates wear and tear on the device socket. The increasing adoption of wireless charging is an outcome of the growing usage of smartphones, tablets, laptops and wearable electronic products such as smartwatches, fit bands and healthcare monitoring equipment.

This breakthrough technology is set to transform the way consumers and industries wirelessly charge and power electronic devices at home, in office, in vehicles and beyond. Samsung, Belkin and Mophie are some of the major players manufacturing wireless chargers that can charge multiple devices in order to provide a greater user experience. In September 2020, Samsung announced the launch of a wireless charging pad that can charge three devices at the same time. The pad supports the Qi wireless charging standard, and other smart devices such as smartphones, earpods and smartwatches are also compatible.

Companies that embrace new technologies for automation, such as mobile robotics with autonomous wireless charging, will be well equipped to meet the demands of the marketplace while bolstering the health, safety and productivity of their workforce.

Wireless charging of electronic devices covers a variety of technologies and transmission ranges used in consumer electronics, healthcare, automotive, industrial and other applications. The overall wireless charging market is expected to be valued at US$4.5 billion in 2021 and is projected to reach US$13.4 billion by 2026, at a CAGR of 24.6 per cent between 2021 and 2026. The growing adoption of wireless technologies in the consumer electronics industry, and the growing sales of EVs are the primary factors contributing to the market growth. Furthermore, the increase in the use of wireless technology to charge warehouse trucks is to create massive opportunities for wireless chargers in the near future.

The radio frequency (RF) charging method is used to wirelessly transfer power to devices. Ossia Inc. is developing a wireless charging device that works over a distance of several feet. The company's Cota technology utilizes RF to send data and power over distances of more than fifteen feet. The transmitters can connect to charge tonnes of mobile devices in an office, coffee shop or other crowded spaces by connecting two Cota ceiling tiles within a radius of a few meters.

The near-field communication (NFC) wireless charging market is projected to grow from US$31.6 million in 2021 to US$1.36 billion by 2026; it is expected to grow at a CAGR of 64.7 per cent during the forecast period.

The NFC wireless charging technology can be incorporated into computer accessories such as touch pen, type cover and mouse if they are equipped with the NFC feature. The use of existing NFC interfaces can be extended for pairing and wireless charging after the standardization of wireless LAN controller (WLC) specifications. In this case, NFC antennas are used to exchange the pairing information and transfer power. For instance, a touch pen incorporated with NFC technology can be charged if it is pressed against a tablet, or a mouse can be charged if placed on a conference table having charging pads. This approach is intuitive, efficient, convenient, flexible and hassle-free as it eliminates the requirement of carrying specific chargers.

With over-the-air charging mechanisms, devices that require charging will need to remain fixed in one place ensuring they have a clear line of sight to the transmitter. According to a report by TechCrunch, Wi-Charge, along with Belkin, is working to launch products that can be charged wirelessly from a distance of ten metres or more.[3] Over-the-air wireless charging will be able to support a broad range of devices, including small, low-power ones such as hearing aids, fitness bands and sensors.

The Federal Communications Commission (FCC) has extended its support for the vision of over-the-air charging. Over-the-air wireless charging is rapidly shifting from a 'nice to have' to a 'need to have' technology. Cesar Johnston, COO and EVP of Engineering at Energous Corporation said in an article, 'Every year, consumers expect more and more from their devices—and an always-charged battery is at the top of their list of expectations. RF wireless charging will make it happen.'[4]

## Use of Drones in Factories

For some parts of the world, drones are not new. Countries like Japan have been using drones, especially for their agricultural sector, for approximately thirty years. However, in the UK, it is a fairly recent phenomenon.[5] Drones have been instrumental and a foundational step in transforming a factory from a traditional one to a smart one. They were initially used for factory surveillance but gradually became an integral part of manufacturing facility.

In October 2021, SEAT S.A. and Eurecat announced that they were testing the use of autonomous drones to transport components within the production line. The pioneering project explores the possibility of using drones to optimize logistics supply. As explained by Alba Gavilán, SEAT S.A. head of digital execution and delivery of production strategy department,[6] the 'goal with this innovation is to explore the advantages of autonomous vertical mobility to clear up space on the floor and shift light-weight parts in a faster, cleaner and more efficient way. In the future, drones could autonomously transport components directly to the line.'

Drones have the ability to accelerate internal delivery processes between production points and can also enhance storage in factories with less space. They are also rapidly replacing the applications of legacy services in the commercial sector, such as aerial surveys, filmography and search and rescue. The main reason for this is the operational ability that can be remotely managed by human operators or even autonomously by onboard computers.

## Collaborative Robots

Smart manufacturing is toggling between Industry 4.0 and Industry 5.0. The latter is largely defined by the new branch of industrial robotics called cobots or collaborative robots. By definition, a cobot is a robot that physically communicates with people in any shared workspace. What differentiates cobots from other industrial robots is that they are designed to work autonomously in an enclosed space.

Deploying cobots also ensures better collaboration. Robots and humans can work together in a flexible and versatile way, while cobots can be tasked with laborious and monotonous work. It will allow people to focus on work that requires knowledge and skills. Cobots are also easy to set up and programme, which further adds to the flexibility, especially in the age of Industry 4.0, where interoperability of robots and automated technologies have become a mainstream feature. Using intuitive software, cobots can be configured and reconfigured with applications for multiple tasks and workflows. It also ensures greater safety. Even though traditional robot arms are extremely powerful, they lack the ability to detect and avoid obstacles. Cobots are the intelligent version that can safely work alongside people by keeping a safe distance from humans. They are also able to keep their distance from dangerous equipment like forklifts.

According to MarketsandMarkets,[7] the cobot segment is projected to grow from US$1.2 billion in 2021 to US$10.5 billion by 2027 at a CAGR of 43.4 per cent. The market is driven by the high return on investment to corporates when using cobots, and its general benefits in terms of competitiveness, boosted production and enhanced quality.

Cobots are also making their mark in the end-consumer segment. In May 2022, a Skyline restaurant in Fairfield appointed a new server that rolls through a twelve-hour shift while treating customers to songs like 'Happy Birthday' and the 'Skyline Time' jingle. 'We (leased) it so that it can help us move food,' said Robin Kurlas, co-owner of the Skyline franchise on Hicks Boulevard.[8] 'The promise of collaborative robots is that they are easier to use. You can get them up and running more quickly. You do not need internal engineering resources. And that they're safe,' said Jeff Burnstein, president of the Association for Advancing Automation, a Michigan-based trade group.

Some of the mundane, time-consuming, labour-intensive yet critical works done by cobots include automated picking, packing, packaging, palletizing and materials handling. The cobots that handle materials easily communicate with other automated solutions in a facility, such as packaging or palletizing. They can also be tasked with the automation of assembly line, machine tending and replenishment.

## The Rise of Automated Guided Vehicles

Automated guided vehicles (AGVs) were initially used as towing trailers to speed up production and were considered just as good-to-have machines that could save time. However, in the late 1990s, when explored further, they were used as a technology that could improve the overall factory conditions. Since then, the market for AGVs has grown rapidly. It continued expanding throughout the twenty-first century and soon became the most common robotic feature across several industry sectors.

These guided computerized vehicles are programmed by software to identify positioning, movement and location. Implementation of AGVs enables just-in-time delivery of raw material, along with computerized control of received assembled parts, and also tracking of shipped articles. Powered by a battery or electric motor, AGVs are now able to take charge of key areas of manufacturing, warehousing, loading and other operations without human interference.

Tony Raggio, general manager of sales at Dematic, the leading supplier of AGVs in Australia and New Zealand, says that it is tailor-designed to navigate any production and warehouse space with a laser guidance system. He adds that their AGVs work as driverless, fully automated forklifts, each with a load capacity of 3,500 kg and a lift height of 4.0 m.[9] These AGVs can also drive themselves onto floor plates at times of inactivity to be charged using the automated opportunity charging function.

The major areas of AGV technology include Towing AGV, Fork AGV, Heavy Load AGV, AGV Robots and AGV Systems. AGVs are supported by high network Wi-Fi enabling direct vehicle-to-vehicle (V2V) and vehicle-to-infrastructure (V2I) communication, while 4G/LTE (long term evolution) systems support additional vehicle-to-network (V2N) connectivity.

The AGV market revenue was at US$2.2 billion in 2021 and is expected to reach US$3.2 billion by 2026, at a CAGR of 7.7 per cent during the forecast period. The growth is largely driven by the demand for automation in material handling across industries. In addition to that, there is also a shift in mass production to mass customization, rising popularity of e-commerce and improved safety standards at workplaces, which are all well-managed by the AGVs.

Vehicle-to-everything, V2X, is the next big step that will unlock the power of AGVs and driverless cars. V2X includes enhanced augmented reality, cooperative driving, extended electronic (NLOS) vision and more precise positioning and, hence, is expected to be a game changer for the industry.

While an AGV is an industrial vehicle that can be pre-programmed to transport goods in a warehouse or manufacturing environment, and guided by magnetic strips or wires installed on or under a warehouse floor, AMR is a vehicle that uses on-board sensors and processors to autonomously move materials without the need for physical guides or markers.[10] It learns its environment, remembers its location and dynamically plans its own path from one destination to another. If its path is blocked, an AMR can reroute itself with no assistance. It can avoid obstacles and unburden workers from repetitive or back-breaking work so the workers can focus on more valuable and fulfilling jobs.

## Future of Semiconductors: AI Chipsets, Power Semiconductors, Photonics

In 2021, the semiconductor market witnessed prominent growth with worldwide semiconductor revenue growing to 25 per cent year-on-year to US$583.5 billion. This was the first time that the market rose beyond the US$500 billion threshold. The growth can be largely attributed to the expanding 5G smartphone market and the continued strength of the worldwide personal computer market.

Semiconductors are the key enablers of products that we use for work, communication, healthcare, travel, entertainment and to make new scientific discoveries and more. In the two years during the COVID-19 pandemic, semiconductor-enabled technologies helped humans operate remotely while staying connected to the world consistently.

The semiconductor industry achieved great successes in 2021 but faced significant challenges, especially with the widespread global semiconductor shortage resulting from the unpredictable rise in demand during the pandemic. The industry saw major fluctuations in chip demand in other industries such as automobiles, which further aggravated the supply–demand imbalance across the world.

In June 2021, the US Senate passed the United States Innovation and Competition Act (USICA), a broad competitiveness legislation that included US$52 billion to bolster domestic chip manufacturing, research and design. The semiconductor industry has urged the US House of Representatives to follow suit and send legislation to the president's desk to be signed into law.[11]

According to a Deloitte report, the chip shortage of the past two years resulted in revenue misses of more than US$500 billion worldwide between the semiconductor and its customer industries, with lost auto sales of more than US$210 billion in 2021 alone.[12]

## AI Chipsets

With AI deepening its strong foothold on the industrial spectrum, the chipsets are set to emerge as a key solution for large-scale data processing. Also known as AI accelerators, these are specialized computer chips meant for high speeds and efficiencies required for large-scale AI-specific calculations. One of the most prominent trends in chip technology is the edge AI chips that help run AI processing 'on the edge', that is, on devices that are not connected to the cloud. Led by edge AI chipsets, the industry is undergoing a significant shift.

With the rising demand for leading-edge AI chipset technologies, many well-financed startups are now posing as strong competitors to market leaders such as Nvidia. For example, Hailo is an Israel-based startup that unveiled a funding round worth US$60 million in March 2020. This was geared towards the rollout of its deep learning chip.

As per MarketsandMarkets, the global AI chipsets market size is expected to be valued at US$7.6 billion in 2020 and is expected to reach US$57.8 billion by 2026, at a CAGR of 40.1 per cent during the forecast period. The key drivers for the market are the increasingly large and complex data sets and the subsequent demand for AI. Other factors that are heightening the demand include its adoption for improving consumer services and reducing operational costs, rise in its applications, improving computing power and an increase in deep learning and neural networks.

## Summary

The manufacturing segment, now mainly considered as 'smart manufacturing' because of the wide range of tech adoptions in recent years, has been one of the key enablers of ground-breaking transformations in various industries across the world. Also known as Industry 4.0, it is the era that has revolutionized the way companies manufacture, enhance and distribute their products. Especially during the pandemic, companies across the world have realized the critical need for embracing the innovations and advancements that this age of industrial revolution has to offer. Companies that want to cope with the advances will have to plan their skilling need as much as their investment in new technologies.

# 5

# Automotive for the People

The next time a rider looks for an Uber, it might just be driverless.

Uber has partnered with Motional, a joint venture between Hyundai and Irish–American automotive supplier Aptiv, to deploy driverless cars.

According to reports, many commuters in Las Vegas have been able to access Motional's robotaxi service through ride-hail companies Lyft and Uber since August and December 2022. The rides are for daytime hours and have always had a human safety operator in the front seat.[1]

Motional and Uber launched their public robotaxi service in Las Vegas in December 2022. For the first time ever, Uber customers were able to hail an autonomous ride using Motional's all-electric Hyundai IONIQ 5-based robotaxis. The service will see Motional's Level 4 autonomous vehicles (AVs) deployed for ride-hail and deliveries on the Uber network in major cities across the US. According to a statement, by Motional, Uber is working with vehicle operators to lay the groundwork for a fully driverless commercial service, with the goal of launching the driverless service to the public in 2023.[2]

The global mobility ecosystem is evolving rapidly and changing the traditional business models of designing, manufacturing, selling, servicing and financing vehicles. Driven by sustainability goals and altering consumer behaviour, the transformations are boosted by the extensive digital innovations of today. From a hardware-dominated industry, automotive is now quickly shifting towards a more software-driven segment. The EVs, connected cars, mobility fleet sharing, CaaS (content as a service) or MaaS (mobility as a service) and onboard sensors are set to become the key features of the automotive industry. Led by cross-sector collaborations, diversifications and unprecedented innovations, the industry will soon be very different from how we have known it or have experienced it till now. According to an article in *Forbes*,[3] industry leaders believe that the future of automotive is not just electric but predominantly a world of intelligent systems maintaining constant interactions with consumers, manufacturers and the new models of supply chains based on software services.

Globally, automated transportation systems are gaining traction. Their use is increasing in cities, both for humans and for freight. Several categories of such systems are visible, being expanded or under consideration in various countries. These include automated bus systems, robotic taxis, automated airport shuttles and in-the-future pilotless flights. Automated urban mass transit includes buses and light trains. Six levels of automation are deployed in buses and light rail systems.

The highest level is fully autonomous and does not require a driver. Other levels include a human driver presence for emergency purposes with high levels of automated features, including sensors to detect objects, collision detection and lane management (for buses). Suburban and light transit trains are considered ideal for automated driverless technology. Many such trains run regularly between airport terminals in cities, such as Zurich, from point to point over short distances and have no need for a driver. Airport transit systems have been the biggest adopter of automated light transit.

Then there is the focus on freight and goods movement where no human interaction is required. The market for automated mass transit is expected to grow significantly in the next few years. For developing countries, the prospect of automated mass transit holds much appeal—they are more affordable for commuters and work better in highly populated markets where roads are already packed with personal vehicles.

According to a MarketsandMarkets report, 'The autonomous train market, in terms of volume, is projected to grow at a CAGR of 4.87 per cent to 2030. It was estimated at 54,558 units in 2017 and is projected to reach 1,06,290 units by 2030.' There are several factors for this: 'The increasing demand for efficient transportation with a high level of safety is expected to drive the market across the globe. The Asia–Pacific region is expected to be the fastest growing market, due to the high adoption of technology, a large number of projects and an increase in government spending towards railway transportation.'

The global automotive industry has added another name to its critical components list and car makers have been struggling due to its shortage—the semiconductors. Until recently, semiconductors were useful mainly in the manufacturing plants of automakers. The use of IoT in the manufacturing value chain depended on the computer chip and semiconductors were not a critical component in vehicles. But now, a significant number of vehicles in the market have a semiconductor embedded in them.

Cars can soon be called mobile devices with wheels. Many of the in-car passenger facilities and engine management systems depend on computer chips. Some of the uses include infotainment systems, collision avoidance systems and even parking assist systems. Touchscreens on the dashboard and the rear seats, speed management, route navigation and other similar systems require the onboard computers in cars to process millions of lines of code every second. The EVs are even more dependent on computer semiconductors for battery management. And with voice assistance, software drivers can now talk their way out of traffic jams.

Self-driving cars may be some years away, but several such features of autonomous vehicles require computer chips. Not surprising that the shortage of semiconductors halted vehicle assembly lines across the world in 2021.

While computer chips make driving and vehicle management more efficient, they also expose the 'mobile on wheels' to the dangers of cyber thievery. Car hacking can be as dangerous as carjacking. Thus, cybersecurity for cars is becoming as important as for other connected devices we use.

'The global automotive cybersecurity market size is projected to grow from US$1.9 billion in 2020 to US$4.0 billion by 2025, at a CAGR of 16.5 per cent,' as per MarketsandMarkets. 'Increased use of electronics per vehicle and a growing number of connected cars, and reinforcement of mandates by regulatory bodies for vehicle data protection are some of the key factors that are driving the market for the automotive cybersecurity market.'

So, what can car hacking do? Hackers can control a car in motion and force it to accelerate or stop suddenly.[5] In one experiment, researchers were able to control various parts of a vehicle using a laptop placed 15 km away. The hackers could change the radio station, turn off the engine and change the temperature setting inside the car. In another example, a hacker based in Australia could hack into an electric car in northern England and steal its data. A fleet of freight trucks can be hijacked or controlled remotely too. Modern freight trucks depend much on connected electronics.

The biggest companies in the automotive world are silently terrified of the potential catastrophe that a car hacker can unleash. This is not just about the car companies alone. Any of the OEM vendors and suppliers that develop software or hardware for the vehicles can be compromised. Car hacking can be worse than carjacking as millions can be impacted in a single attack.

The industry is transforming rather radically. Reports suggest that the market for connected cars is set to grow by US$117.34 billion from 2020 to 2025, at a CAGR of 26.26 per cent.[4] The AR would grow at a CAGR of 17.60 per cent from 2020 to 2025.[6] Around 25 per cent of the cars sold by 2025 will have electric engines, though most of them would be hybrids, and 95 per cent of cars will still depend on fossil fuels for at least part of their power.[7] Other rapidly expanding genres include autonomous self-driving cars, ultra-classic airbags and cars with energy-storing body panels.

Keeping sustainability at the core, the automotive industry is also steering through massive evolutions in the entire product life cycle. Today, manufacturers need to not only leverage smarter technologies and data-driven processes in the design-development stage but also try to stay connected with automobiles that have gone out of the showroom. This is mainly to understand the changes in usage patterns that can help update the next line of products and service offerings. Car makers are keeping a laser-sharp focus on building customer centricity, superior connectivity with mobility services, strong digital supply chains and adaptation to the emergence of a changing workforce in order to maintain their competitive edge.

Let us look at some of the major technological highlights of the automotive industry today.

## End-to-End Automotive Software Platforms: Core of Automotive Soon

As mentioned earlier, cars of the future will soon be like supercomputers on wheels as the sector is fast moving away from being hardware-defined to a software-defined mobility platform. To successfully equip a vehicle with the latest features such as onboard infotainment, electrification, self-driving abilities and advanced driver assistance systems, it is now critical for automakers to possess better quality software systems that ensure seamless integration among vehicle subsystems and security systems. In line with it, General Motors announced the launch of Ultifi in 2023, an end-to-end software platform for vehicles. It will be built on top of the company's vehicle intelligence platform, or VIP, which is the base of the hardware architecture, and will provide greater data processing power.[8] Today, carmakers are not just beginning to develop software in-house but are also working towards having their own vehicle-dedicated operating systems and computer processors.[9] Reports suggest that software complexity is on track to nearly triple over the next ten years.[10]

## Technologies Set to Bolster the Electric Vehicle Revolution

The automotive sector is consistently working towards innovative technologies that would facilitate and ensure a faster shift towards EVs, in the fifth industrial revolution.[11] One of the biggest challenges in EV adoption currently is its battery range and the lack of charging infrastructure. Some of the developments to address this have been as follows.

## Adoption of Different Battery Technology

From sodium-ion, manganese, to zinc-ion and others, OEMs are looking for the perfect ingredient with an appropriate mix of scalability and costs as the focus is on making batteries last longer.

## Wireless Charging

Using inductive charging technology, much like wireless charging works on smartphones and appliances, EVs can get charged just by standing on certain spots.

## Electrified Roads

This is the possibility of using overhead cables for charging.

## Battery Swapping

Battery swapping is a new technology that allows EV owners to change their used or spent batteries with a fully charged one. They can stop at a station or keep an extra one at home.

This system will allow people to carry extra batteries or change them even in long distance travel in EVs.[12]

## Ultra-Fast Charging

The development of standardized chargers will bring with it the added benefit of making charging much faster than before.

## Safety Innovations in Intelligent Mobility

The demand for advanced and innovative safety features such as blind-spot detection and panoramic rear views is rising steadily. Here, AR and connected cars are the two major innovations that are propelling the safety aspect of future mobility and gradually making 5G connectivity the future of the automotive industry. Experts believe that 5G is set to redefine mobility as we know it. Adding to that is the V2X communication system, which enables a consistent flow of information between vehicles, pedestrians and other road infrastructure.[13] It alerts the drivers about nearby hazards and diminishes the chances of accidents. It would significantly improve road safety around the world. Another latest safety feature is the occupancy status (OS) technology. OS is a detection technology that is able to identify the occupant's behaviour.[14] It monitors occupant positioning and occupancy behaviour and ensures safety during changing environments while giving an overall comfortable and safe experience to the passengers. The members of the Alliance of Automobile Manufacturers and the Association of Global Automakers are keen to incorporate occupancy monitoring as a standard feature by 2025.

## Smart Manufacturing and Repair

According to a report by Capgemini, the automotive sector—as compared to any other sector—has been the most enthusiastic to adopt smart factories. It has made remarkable investments to propagate digital manufacturing operations. The report revealed that 'smart factories could add up to US$160 billion annually to the global auto industry in productivity gains by 2023 onwards.'[15] Some of the technologies that are already bolstering the automotive manufacturing space widely include AI and machine learning (ML), both for vehicle designing and manufacturing. Robots have been in the industry for decades, however, AI-powered robots known as collaborative robots or cobots are now redefining the manufacturing landscape completely.[16] Then there is 3D printing. The automotive industry is also second in line to use additive manufacturing for production and 3D printing to fabricate parts. It is now an essential and established technology in the auto space. With digital twin, manufacturers are able to optimize every phase of their production process. AR assists in optimizing the assembly process making it quicker, reducing errors, ensuring a safe environment for the workers and reducing the cost of manufacturing of prototypes. With AR, automotive technicians are able to perform complex repairs and maintenance to vehicles more accurately and quickly. Big data and data analytics help in gathering information from vehicles which are then analysed for predictive maintenance, informing managers about their fleets and sending alerts to concerned authorities in the case of accidents.

## Transforming Supply Chain

The tech-driven automotive scenario, along with the shift towards shared mobility and the impact of the COVID-19 pandemic on the sector, have made traditional OEMs face a series of challenges in the race to keep up with the transitions. OEMs and suppliers are pressed with the need to optimize cash conversion, invest in new business models and look at divestments. Some of the trends that are posing a challenge for the OEMs include:[17] technology-related portfolio shifts that are pushing OEMs to focus on e-motor technologies and battery innovations rather than suspension, wheels and engine systems; competition from new OEM entrants with high levels of automation; and sustainability goals and costs attached to implement the planned transformations.

For traditional OEMs, the challenge is two-pronged. On the one hand, they are struggling to balance their priorities of consolidation, boost financial performance and improve operational efficiencies, but on the other hand, they need to build capabilities to stay at par with the MaaS world. As a result, in the past few years, traditional OEMs have been collaborating with their industry counterparts and the leaders to share the costs and risks of addressing the ever-changing market.

Examples include a US$1.13 billion mobility partnership between Daimler and BMW where they aim to provide their sixty million customers a 360° seamless experience of sustainability, car-sharing, ride-hailing, parking, charging and multimodal transport services; and then Waymo's partnership with Renault and Nissan to introduce driverless transportation-as-a-service offerings in France and Japan.

The automotive industry depends largely on the supply chain for timely production processes. For example, the US car industry is highly dependent on Chinese parts and had recorded a spending of more than US$1.5 billion in 2018. A robust digital supply chain and a detailed planning process can ensure a 10 per cent reduction in manufacturing costs, a 4 per cent improvement in volume throughput and an 11 per cent faster response time in line with the demands.[18] In 2022, the digital twin supply chain management witnessed more use cases. It helped bridge the gaps across systems and propagated a better understanding of the factors of supply chains so that businesses could adapt accordingly.[19]

## Startups/New Entrants Setting the Tone for the Industry

Several new entrants are further redefining the sector with unique products that comply with the four key automotive trends: electrification, connectivity, autonomous and shared mobility.

The promising startups of 2022 as mentioned by StartUs Insights included Intvo, an organization developing pedestrian behaviour technology, NoTraffic connecting drivers with city roadways and helping them manage various traffic-related challenges with its AI-powered traffic signal platform and aqueduct charging system by ChargeX, which offered a modular EV charging solution that can convert parking spaces into charging stations. Another organization called Beam is focusing on e-scooters to promote shared mobility in the Asia–Pacific region. The e-scooters use an aviation-grade aluminium frame and are customized for sharing, safety, reliability and durability.

## A Consumer's Perspective

The influx of technologies embedded in the car will subsequently make UI/UX (user interface and user experience) design a part of a car designer's toolkit. Consumers will eventually make cars a living space where they can dedicate their freed-up time to other personal activities or consume novel forms of media and services. Along with the constant updates and information on the latest technologies, consumers would also demand consistent upgradability of their vehicles.

The 2022 Deloitte Global Automotive Consumer Study states that while there has been a substantial increase in the virtual automotive purchase process, ensuring ease of buying and convenience, consumers still prefer to purchase a vehicle at an authorized dealership. AR is also redefining the buying experience of consumers. Virtual showrooms are increasingly the way buyers prefer their car shopping experience to be. With the technology, consumers are presented with options such as virtual try-ons at many online retail shops.[20] Customers can opt for try-on glasses before ordering a car.

## Emergence of Autonomous Ride-Sharing

Leading companies such as Waymo (US), General Motors (US), Nissan (Japan) and Volvo (Sweden) are heavily investing in the development of self-driving cars. Autonomous cars (Level 4 and Level 5) and semiautonomous cars (Level 1, Level 2 and Level 3) are expected to drive the development of new mobility models and provide opportunities for infrastructural development. Governments of the US, Germany, China, Singapore, Sweden, France, Japan and Norway have already relaxed the legal hindrances for testing self-driving vehicles.

According to industry experts, the introduction of self-driving vehicles for shared mobility services will help reduce the cost of ownership and improve fleet management. These self-driving vehicles are expected to provide a safe, convenient and economical mode of transportation in the future. Thus, OEMs, autonomous driving system providers and fleet managers are focusing on launching autonomous shared mobility services such as robotic taxi, ride-sharing and ride-hailing. OEMs such as Ford, Toyota, and Volkswagen; tier 1 suppliers such as Bosch, Continental, ZF, Aptiv and Denso; and governments from several countries are increasingly investing in the development of autonomous vehicle technology and commercial mobility with the help of autonomous vehicles.

Self-driving cars are currently based on the level of human intervention required to operate the vehicles. The levels as defined by the Society of Automotive Engineers (SAE) International and the US National Highway Traffic Safety Administration (NHTSA) range from zero to five (0–5), where 0 is completely manually controlled and 5 is a completely autonomous vehicle. Level 0 technically implies that the vehicle ought to be completely controlled by the driver, and the vehicle does not provide any driver assistance on its own. Levels 1 to 3 offer semiautonomy within the vehicle by offering advanced driver-assistance system features such as adaptive cruise control (ACC) and lane centring. These technologies reduce human intervention and mitigate the risks of accidents that can be caused by human errors.

A few of the key OEMs that offer semiautonomous cars are General Motors, Daimler, Volkswagen AG and Tesla. Today, numerous OEMs are offering Level 1 and Level 2 semiautonomous cars and are planning to increase the number of models with Level 1 and Level 2 safety features to create differentiated products and match up to their competitor's offerings. In March 2021, Honda showcased its first Level 3 semiautonomous car. The company is planning to manufacture a batch of around 100 cars initially for lease. OEMs such as Hyundai, Mercedes-Benz and BMW are planning to launch Level 3 semiautonomous cars by 2022.

According to the definition set by SAE, autonomous cars, which include Level 4 and Level 5 self-driving cars, do not require a driver to be present in the vehicle. These vehicles rely on cutting-edge technologies including sensors and actuators for primary inputs such as monitoring nearby vehicles and obstacles and also use ML systems and complex algorithms to process these inputs. The processed inputs are then used to plot a path and guide the vehicle by sending timely instructions to the vehicle's actuators that control the vehicle's acceleration, braking and steering. The advanced parking feature includes hands-free parking, controlling steering, acceleration, braking and gear changes when parallel parking or backing into a parking space. A surround-view camera is used to help with advanced parking features while parking. The camera unit and ultrasonic sensors are used to sense the surrounding environment of the cars.

The combination of these systems embedded in autonomous cars eliminates the need for a driver to be present in the vehicle at all—a major differentiating factor between autonomous and semiautonomous vehicles. Other main OEMs that are developing or have launched autonomous cars include Waymo, Baidu, Ford and PSA Group.

Asia–Pacific is playing a vital role in the growth of semiautonomous cars, whereas North America and European regions are pivotal in the growth of the autonomous cars market. OEMs in China, Japan and South Korea are offering a number of car models with Level 1 and Level 2 semiautonomous features. For instance, in 2021, Toyota launched Lexus LS and Toyota Mirai models with Level 2 safety features.

OEMs in the Asia–Pacific region, such as Hyundai, Kia, Nissan, Honda, SAIC, Geely and Mahindra, are also focusing on offering car models with Level 1 and Level 2 features. Europe is home to leading luxury car manufacturers such as BMW, Audi, Porsche, Mercedes-Benz, Volvo and Maserati. Most of these are working to add various features of autonomous driving. Many cars, trucks and SUVs offer some Level 1 and Level 2 autonomous vehicle features. Consumers will soon get many new upgraded features like adaptive cruise control with stop-go, lane centring, lane following, automatic overtaking, and traffic sign recognition.[21]

The US is one of the leaders in autonomous car development and investment.

Waymo became the first service provider to offer driverless taxi rides to the public in the US in 2020. Although there is no driver in the car, the vehicles still have remote human overseers. In January 2021, the US exempted some of the crash standards for automated vehicles that are designed to carry only goods, not people, to remove barriers for the deployment of autonomous cars. In 2021, Ford Motor Company, Argo AI and Walmart collaborated to launch an autonomous vehicle delivery service in Miami, Austin and Washington, D.C.[22]

Countries in the rest of the world have also taken significant initiatives to promote the adoption of self-driving cars in their domestic market. For example, in October 2017, Saudi Crown Prince Mohammed bin Salman announced an investment of around US$500 billion to invest by 2030 in the Neom economic zone smart city project, which will further promote the use of autonomous vehicles in the country.

Saudi Arabia also announced to have 30 per cent EVs by 2030 and eliminate planet-warming emissions by 2060. Saudi Arabia has invested in Lucid Motors, California, which will develop EVs and hardware for autonomous technologies in the future. In 2021, Metals Group Australia also made an investment worth US$3 billion in the country to process minerals used in EV batteries.

Countries such as Brazil, Argentina and South Africa are also making efforts to develop self-driving car technology and the required infrastructure. For example, AGVS, an autonomous vehicle technology developer in Brazil with a portfolio of self-guided vehicles, has started using the radio frequency identification (RFID) technology of another Brazilian company, eSolutech (Brazil), to gain more competitiveness.

Minimal road accidents and human safety are critical factors for the development of advanced vehicle technologies. Some governments have implemented regulations that mandate OEMs to incorporate safety features such as intelligent speed assistance, emergency stop signals, reversing detection systems and supplementary features. The adoption of technologies would support the growth of semiautonomous cars and a gradual transition from semiautonomous to autonomous vehicles in the future.

Key market players across the globe have also invested significantly in developing supporting technologies for self-driving cars. For example, in 2020, Cruise, a startup owned by GM, announced its electric self-driving vehicle, Origin, in the US. The vehicle does not have traditional controls such as pedals and provides more space for passengers. Similarly, in Europe, in 2019, Audi announced joining an alliance with Daimler and BMW to develop an advanced driving assistance system. In Asia–Pacific, major automotive players such as Toyota and Nissan have significantly invested and partnered with other players for the growth of self-driving cars.

Similarly, in 2019, Hyundai announced that it would invest US$17 billion over the next six years in new technologies to help make the switch to electric and autonomous vehicles. In April 2021, Woven Planet, a subsidiary of Toyota, acquired Lyft's self-driving unit, Level 5, for US$550 million. Lyft has a transportation network that is uniquely capable of scaling autonomous vehicles. Likewise, in July 2021, Ford announced joining the Lyft ride-hailing service to offer its autonomous rides on the Lyft network by 2022.

Autonomous vehicles operating with little or no human intervention vehicles are the next big thing in mobility. The goal is to reduce accidents caused due to human errors, reduce traffic congestion, facilitate hassle-free transport and make commute time more productive.

Furthermore, the development of autonomous vehicles is set to drive the growth of ride sharing. According to the *Future of Driving* report from Ohio University, with the use of autonomous taxis, the waiting time for a cab would come down from an average of five minutes to just thirty-six seconds. Moreover, autonomous ride-sharing will make the cost come down to just US$0.5 per mile. For instance, according to secondary research, a ride-hailing company's per ride charges are approximately US$2 per mile, of which it takes about 50 cents and US$1.50 is with the driver. For an autonomous car or robotic taxi instead of a driver-driven car, it can straightaway charge a customer about US$1 per mile and earn an additional 50 cents per mile. However, the overhead costs such as the maintenance of a car, navigation and payment services would be a part of it. Autonomous cars would also solve the problem of first and last mile accessibility. This means the cars should be able to drive autonomously from door to door, negotiating traffic and small roads in suburbs. The autonomous features will not just be for regulated driving conditions of highways. Public transportation usage suffers from a variety of issues that decrease the number of potential riders that ultimately choose an alternative form of transportation to get to their destination. 'One of these challenges, known as the first mile/last mile (FM/LM) problem, is the requirement of the rider to get from the starting point of their journey to the place of transportation, which in turn requires another leg of their journey from the transportation station to their destination,' a University of Michigan paper says.

Autonomous vehicles will be able to offer door to door transport mobility as they mature.[23]

Autonomous vehicles are still in the development stages. Many OEMs have working prototypes, which are being tested in different regions. Many companies are competing with each other to bring a fully autonomous vehicle to the market. These include Lyft, Ford, Uber, Honda, Toyota and Tesla. Waymo, the autonomous vehicle division of Alphabet, Google's parent company, has begun testing trip fares with its early riders as it moves closer to launching its commercial ride-sharing service in

Phoenix, Arizona. Considering these factors, the development of autonomous vehicles will drive the ride-sharing market by 2030.

## Autonomous Vehicles and Connectivity

The race to launch a fully autonomous car is gaining momentum, as technology companies such as Apple and Waymo are competing with car companies such as Audi, Tesla and Ford and ride-sharing companies such as Lyft and Uber to overcome technical challenges and enable an entirely new way of driving. However, before attempting to launch autonomous vehicles, the industry leaders need to master connectivity protocols to deliver V2X capabilities. There are several components of V2X, including vehicle-to-vehicle (V2V), vehicle-to-infrastructure (V2I), vehicle-to-pedestrian (V2P) and vehicle-to-cloud (V2C) communications. In this multifaceted ecosystem, cars will talk to each other, to infrastructure such as traffic lights or parking spaces and to smartphone-toting pedestrians and data centres via cellular networks.

The V2P communication involves the detection of a pedestrian on or near the road. V2P detection systems can be implemented in a vehicle to provide an alert to drivers. In V2P communication, a pedestrian uses an alert system, which is a hand-held device such as a smartphone or smartwatch that will enable information exchange between the pedestrian and the vehicle.

The V2I connectivity is the wireless exchange of critical operational data between a vehicle and infrastructure, intended to not only mitigate vehicle crashes but also enable a wide range of other safety, mobility and environmental benefits. The V2I communication technology applies to all vehicle types and roads and transforms the infrastructure equipment into smart infrastructure through the incorporation of algorithms.

These algorithms use data exchanged between vehicles and infrastructure elements to perform calculations that can recognize high-risk positions in advance and alert the drivers.

V2V communication is the wireless exchange of data among vehicles traveling in the vicinity, which offers opportunities for significant safety improvements. The V2V connectivity approach is most suited for the short-range vehicular network. Emergency brake light warning, forward collision warning, intersection movement assist, blind spot and lane change warning, do-not-pass warning and control loss warning are common V2V communication functions.

## Summary

People will continue to move but the machines that transport us will become far more independent than today and will take many decisions on their own. Before self-driving in personal vehicles, mass transport will become highly automated. At one level, it will be highly personalized with driver preferences loaded in each vehicle, while mass transport may no longer be a collective movement. Personal pod taxis and other such innovations could create new transport solutions. Fuel shifts and highly connected vehicles will impact design and manufacturing as well as freight systems. The automotive sector promises to be safer, greener and smarter.

# 6

# Vectors of Changing Sectors

Technology advancements have been reshaping industries across sectors for almost two decades. But a much-accelerated rate of digital adoption has been witnessed in the past couple of years owing to the COVID-19 pandemic. With this digital boom, there have been several sectoral-specific shifts that are consistently altering the business models of a range of industries. Chemical sciences and process automation have applications everywhere. There are, however, sector-specific shifts that are changing the business models of a range of industries. From transport to textiles, every sector is getting defined by connectivity and is data-driven.

Several sub-verticals within the sectors are also shifting in unimaginable ways. If roads are getting smarter, so are cars. If cars are smarter, so are accident-prevention systems. Mobile phone systems will be transformed by 5G and 6G connectivity. Not just the manufacturing but textiles themselves are getting smart. Business leaders will soon find that spying technology is a bigger worry than supply chain challenges.

In this chapter, we will do a detailed examination into some of the sectors that have had major breakthroughs in the recent past and are expected to reinvent themselves completely in the coming future.

## Highways

With a set of smart technologies, our roads are becoming smarter and more efficient and with it, their entire ecosystem—ranging from construction and maintenance to traffic management. For example, in the case of EVs, to overcome the challenge of limited battery charge, we are constructing smart roads and highways that can help charge EVs easily. Power cables are being embedded under the roads to charge EVs driving over it. The roads are now getting equipped to energize a car and experimental technologies are also exploring ways to trap energy even from passing vehicles.

Sensor-embedded smart roads can monitor traffic, weather conditions and general status such as a breach or damage, wherein the sensors can automatically alert highway-management authorities. The key element of high-tech highways is their ability to converse with vehicles. Smart vehicles with their own set of sensors will share constant information with roads that will help drivers make better decisions on navigation and traffic management and allow highway management plan better.

The National Highway Authority of India (NHAI) is infusing the use of technology in several activities including construction, road condition surveys, electronic toll systems and project team management. By deploying a cloud-based and AI-powered big data analytics platform called Data Lake, the entire project-management workflow of NHAI has now been transformed from manual to online portals. From project documentation to contractual decisions, all the approvals are done via the portal. Every contractor and project team has been mandated to work on the portal.

'NHAI undertook safety audit of 16,500 km of national highways through safety auditors specialized in safe roads engineering studies and safety audit of 19,300 km has been completed during this financial year till December 2022,' the Ministry of Road Transport and Highways of India said. Over 260 safety audit reports have been uploaded by safety consultants which are monitored for implementation by the highway regulator.[1]

This works to ensure the regular flow of information regarding its various projects and also predicts the financial outcomes.

The next key development in smart highways is the rise of automated toll management, important for financial margins and improved efficiency for drivers. FASTag deploys Radio Frequency Identification (RFID) technology to collect tolls.

Experts say that the data generated from automated toll collections will be a goldmine for planning and designing highways in the future. NHAI's subsidiary Indian Highways Management Company is embarking on a global navigation satellite system-based tolling project. Using global satellite-based technology implies that toll plazas will directly be in contact with the vehicle's navigation devices. Once they are matched with tolling and payment systems effectively, the vehicle will pay the toll plaza directly every time it passes through a checkpoint. To make the most of satellite-based toll or parking charges, the vehicle makers will have to include an onboard unit that is compatible with the relevant systems. Total toll collection through FASTag on fee plazas, including state highway tolls, increased 46 per cent to Rs 500 billion in 2022. Countries like India are using a range of simple to complex technologies to achieve efficiency at scale and speed.[2]

Digitally enabled smart highways are being used across the world in different ways. Sensors embedded in the roads can monitor traffic and road conditions. Similarly, glow-in-the-dark roads can ensure that energy is not needlessly spent in lighting up remote stretches. Interactive lighting can complement solar light, which is responsive to movement and visibility conditions.

Roads and highways are at the intersection of two sectors: smart cities and smart mobility. The best results can be obtained with a view of the interconnectedness of mobility and city life. As policymakers and entrepreneurs deploy technology across sectors, keeping the big picture in mind would form the essence of it.

Smart roads will work best with smart vehicles. Both sectors will have to work together to achieve the most out of technological innovations.

## The New Era of Mobile and 5G Network

Time lag in connectivity is reducing to near-zero levels as the speed and strength of communications technology is getting enhanced. The year 2022 may well be remembered as one when 5G matured. More than 205 operators in eighty countries and territories launched 5G mobile services during this period. And 493 operators in 150 countries and territories were investing in 5G, including trials, acquisition of licences, planning, network deployment and launches, according to GSA. While each country is not completely covered internally, the process is accelerating. In previous years, 5G was run as a pilot project in various countries. Just about thirty-eight countries had at least one region with 5G service in mid-2020.[3]

The 5G network is not just evolving rapidly but also combining to create new ecosystems. The industrial metaverse has emerged as one such fascinating ecosystem. A collection of uniquely configured technologies are allowing immersive digital experiences for not just consumers but for producers too—enabled by high-speed connectivity.

In simple terms, a metaverse is a digital or virtual version of the real world. These exist in many different parts—from a gaming console that replicates a car race to a virtual reality (VR) headset where a person can walk around in a digital landscape. A metaverse happens when many such parts are combined for a specific action or activity. For example, a 3D version of a machine can be seen on a computer. With a VR headset, one can walk around it. In a metaverse situation, not just the machine but an entire factory can be created digitally for walkthroughs and production planning. The images inside the metaverse can be interactive and powered by AI and edge computing while being connected by 5G speeds.

The applications are tremendous. NASA revealed in 2022 that it has conducted a 'holoportation', a combination of teleporting a hologram. The deployment of holoportation allows users to see, hear and interact with remote participants in 3D as if they are actually present in the same physical space. 'Using the Microsoft Hololens Kinect camera and a personal computer with custom software from Aexa, ESA (European Space Agency) astronaut Thomas Pesquet had a two-way conversation with live images of (two doctors) in the middle of the International Space Station. This was the first holoportation handshake from Earth in space,' NASA said.

This technology has been experimented with for some years and now is reaching maturity while triggering opportunities for various applications, mostly because of improved connectivity. After such experiments, it is not difficult to imagine doctors advising patients or engineers resolving problems in remote locations.

Creating digital versions also helps companies reduce quality issues in manufacturing. Boeing and Airbus have declared that they will design the next generation of their airplanes in the digital metaverse. This means they will create and simulate every aspect of designing, manufacturing and testing digitally ahead of the actual production. With the rollout of 5G, metaverse and related applications will be accelerated across the industrial spectrum. High-speed connectivity and low latency are critical for any real-time application and usage. Companies using metaverse-based solutions will also have to change their internal business and manufacturing processes. If many of the design and quality-check issues are avoided with digital design, then numerous physical steps may become redundant.

Andreas Müller, head of communication and network technology at Bosch Corporate Research, says, 'For the first time, a mobile communications standard has been developed that focuses not on connecting people, but on the communication between sensors, devices, machines, and more on the so-called internet of things.' The main highlight of 5G is that it allows a data transfer rate of twenty gigabits a second,[4] which is approximately twenty times faster than what was provided by 4G.

In addition to speed that would propagate faster gaming or movie downloading, it would also ensure greater security. 'Even applications that have to work absolutely reliably and securely can be realized wirelessly with 5G. This applies, for example, to a remotely operated crane as well as to a manufacturing facility,' Müller added. 5G will also usher in new possibilities for augmented reality and VR experiences via a handset, be that gaming, entertainment or advertising.

Then there is the advent of Wi-Fi 6. This network technology will bring ultra-efficiency to wireless connectivity. According to Cisco, 'Wi-Fi 6, also known as 802.11ax, is changing the way we connect and consume information. The Wi-Fi 6 standard builds on the strengths of earlier Wi-Fi standards while improving efficiency, flexibility and scalability. These enhancements provide new and existing networks with increased speed and capacity for next-generation applications ... It also provides more predictable performance for advanced applications such as 4K or 8K video, high-density, high-definition collaboration apps, all-wireless offices, and the internet of things.'[5]

With this, our dependence on mobile phones just keeps increasing. Consequently, there has been a concomitant rise in fraud using mobile phones. Hundreds of millions of new users joining the digital mainstream are easier to defraud as they are vulnerable to sophisticated scams. Apart from individuals, even enterprises are placing more and more reliance on mobile-based business processes, as was seen especially during the pandemic period.

The global GSM Association (GSMA) in its *Global Mobile Trends 2021* report has predicted a huge rise in services beyond the core of fixed and mobile connectivity: 'Since 2017, there has been a notable increase in the range of online services people use in developing countries, including education, healthcare and e-government. The breadth of mobile internet usage is likely to increase further resulting from COVID-19.... Services beyond core include a range of B2C and B2B services, such as pay TV, media and advertising, the internet of things, cloud, security, financial and lifestyle services, and solutions for vertical industries.'

Not surprisingly, the scope and extent of fraud on mobile usage has increased dramatically. Global efforts are being made to curb it. GSMA has developed a new international fraud deterrent system with Mobileum. The aim of the trial is to evaluate advanced collaborative fraud and nuisance call-prevention techniques. The effort will involve using technology for call path-tracing to find the disguised source of a call, live threat monitoring and alerts for providing a real-time view and warnings about active fraud campaigns, an address book for providing an authenticated list of network identifiers and call validation to confirm the provenance of a call.

All these steps will prevent and investigate robo-calling or automated calls that can lead to fraud like SIM swapping. The US communications regulator has assessed that such fraudulent robotic calls cost US$10 billion every year. As mobile-based financial transactions rise, so do cases of fraud.

To combat fraud, new and emerging technologies can be brought into play. French firm Thales has launched biometric advanced voice authentication technology for mobile phone operators and users. 'The voices of the callers are quickly matched against the stored voiceprints of known scammers and individuals with suspicious call patterns,' says Thales.

Transaction monitoring software is being used by banks to track usage patterns by consumers. Such software can assess if a mobile transaction fits a pattern or is unusual. Suspicious transactions can raise red flags for the users and service providers. Preventing mobile-based fraud will require coordinated efforts between several institutions including banking and telecom regulators, industry bodies representing mobile operators, banking and financial services and security technology providers. This is especially important for emerging markets where mobile usage is growing exponentially.

Apart from individual users, the enterprise of usage of telecom services exposes the companies to mobile fraud as well. Awareness of cybersecurity has focused a lot on networks and broadband-based connectivity. Now, emerging technology is being used to tackle mobile-connectivity-based frauds.

## Cybersecurity

Technological innovations have reinvented and transformed the cybersecurity market infrastructure completely. Advancements such as zero trust, security orchestration, automation and response (SOAR), secure access service edge (SASE) and extended detection and response (XDR) are the way forward for the cybersecurity landscape. In real-world systems, organizations may have their entire solution developed on upcoming cybersecurity technologies, which will decide the complexity of the security solutions being developed and the levels of security that will have to be built in.

Zero trust is a cybersecurity strategy wherein security policy is applied based on a context established through least-privileged access controls and strict user authentication. In the post-COVID-19 scenario, the global zero-trust security market size is projected to grow from US$19.6 billion in 2020 to US$51.6 billion by 2026, with a CAGR of 17.4 per cent.

Rapid digital transformations in society have intensified cyber threats by many folds. Especially post the COVID-19 crisis, it is bringing in new challenges that require adaptive and innovative responses. Several internal and external policies are being put in place to combat such effects. For example, the UK government has invested in a range of initiatives to help cybersecurity startups, early-stage companies and high-growth companies develop market-leading products and secure external investments. There are over 200 firms with cybersecurity initiatives supported by governments.

Regulatory implications such as General Data Protection Regulation (GDPR), Federal Information Security Management Act (FISMA), Payment Card Industry Data Security Standard (PCI-DSS), and Health Insurance Portability and Accountability Act (HIPAA) have been evolving to help organizations achieve regulatory compliances.

Based on components, the cybersecurity market is segmented into hardware, software and services. The cybersecurity technology is now offered by various vendors as an integrated platform or a tool that consolidates an enterprise's existing infrastructure. Vendors also offer cybersecurity hardware associated with services that help organizations in implementing the required solution in their current infrastructure.

According to MarketsandMarkets, the cybersecurity market was valued at US$217.87 billion in 2021 and is projected to grow from US$240.27 billion in 2022 to US$345.38 billion by 2026, exhibiting a CAGR of 9.5 per cent from 2022 to 2026. The major factors that are pushing the cybersecurity market include the rising frequency and sophistication of target-based cyberattacks, increasing demand for the cybersecurity mesh and growing demand for cyber-savvy boards.

It is critical for cybersecurity infrastructure to evolve according to the technological landscape and increasingly sophisticated cyber threats. For instance, VPN technology does not provide significant security against cyber threats because it lacks network segmentation and traffic visibility, is unsuitable for dynamic networks and lacks Wi-Fi security. Eventually, conventional methods such as software composition analysis (SCA) tool will disappear as these tools do not scale due to constant friction stemming from false-positives and false-negatives.

The next gen firewall was designed to have a deep packet inspection of encrypted and unencrypted traffic, but these products have become increasingly difficult to operate and manage, often leveraging separate and loosely integrated solutions to tackle different threats and compliance requirements.

The software-defined perimeter (SDP) is an emerging technology that is changing cloud networking. SDP provides a holistic solution to remove the reliance on hardware across the entire security stack and to deploy, manage and visualize network connections using only software.

DevOps native tools are the embracing tools that use component intelligence that enables automation at a higher scale. It is also modernizing governance and eliminating manual processes.

Within cybersecurity the focus on cloud is a distinct segment. With every industry witnessing digital proliferation, organizations have started formulating strategies to converge IT and operational technology (OT) environments at the technological, security and process levels. Due to IT/OT convergence, IT and OT can jointly address security issues, leading to an integrated approach that provides enhanced security against intrusions occurring externally and trying to attack the central security governance throughout the company. As a result, the growing use of bring your own device (BYOD), choose your own device (CYOD), company owned/personally enabled (COPE) and company owned/business only (COBO) are the major factors propelling the growth of the cloud security market.

The overall cloud security market size, by security type, is expected to grow from US$40.8 billion in 2021 to US$77.5 billion by 2026 at a CAGR of 13.7 per cent during the forecast period, as per MarketsandMarkets.

Based on security types, the cloud security market is segmented into perimeter security, network security, endpoint security, application security and data security. Various vendors offer cloud security solutions as an integrated platform or a tool that integrates with enterprises' existing infrastructure. Vendors also offer cloud security hardware associated with services that help organizations implement the required solution in their existing infrastructures. Several developments have been witnessed in cybersecurity software and related hardware development kits in recent years. The network security segment is expected to dominate the cloud security market with US$6.6 billion in 2021 and is projected to grow at a 13.1 per cent CAGR.

'The more connected we are, the more vulnerable we are to hackers trying to penetrate these networks. We saw a 33 per cent increase between 2020 and 2021 in ransomware alone. With the rise of software-based models and increased connectivity, vulnerabilities are greater,' says Marisa Viveros, vice president, strategy and offerings, IBM. 'To mitigate these risks, companies are producing technologies with embedded security and educating programmers and architects to invest in security from the ground up. It is also important the public is educated on using software more responsibly and to be vigilant about phishing emails or messages on social media that can access bank information or sensitive personal data.'

The global cloud security market by application is primarily segmented into visibility and risk assessment and user and data governance, activity monitoring and analytics and threat protection and remediation/mitigation. The other cloud security solutions and services applications include disaster recovery management and business continuity plan.

## Garments and Textiles Industry

The age of mass customization is being driven by predictive technologies that can anticipate, plan and produce for each consumer's specific needs. This is particularly relevant to the global readymade garment industry.

Irrespective of age, gender or geography, the first question for a consumer is whether a particular garment's size will fit or not. Being in vogue is important but wearing the right fit is essential. Global designers and clothing brands are increasingly using sophisticated tech tools to clothe their customers with the right fit. The industry faces a return rate of 20–40 per cent because buyers find that their clothes do not fit. Add to this the fact that the size nomenclature differs in various countries. Often the US and Europe size system does not account for the body shapes of people in other countries.

A full-body 3D scanner will automatically gather body measurements and capture images. This will help extract error-free data in a manner that will not possibly be done by hand. Each such scan will take about ten seconds. Global brands are already leaning on AI and 3D scanning to improve the size of sportswear, casuals and clothes for children. Berlin-based Fit Analytics works with global brands to help their shoppers choose the right fit. Consumers can use an online size advisor where they have to select their preferences. A customer can say that they have a slightly curvy belly and need a tight shoulder fit while adding their height and weight. A series of images can help the consumer select the right configuration for their specific body shape following which the machine learning (ML) algorithm will suggest the correct size for that consumer. With the help of these data, clothing companies can also create more options within a size category. Another such company, WAIR, based in California says it has the world's largest network of 3D body scanners that has helped it get over two million scans. 'Over 3,000 3D body scanners operating in 55 countries are used to continuously capture validated 3D body scans. Over 400 body measurements are processed from each scan and users enter enriched personal information,' says WAIR.

For young startups who want to take on legacy players, New York-based Shapeways can help design and create customized clothing with 3D printers. With the use of 3D printers, designers are able to become entrepreneurs with minimal investment in manufacturing facilities. More importantly, they can offer precision fitting using body shape data for consumer categories, which get left out from mass market products.

While predictive analysis of trends has helped the fashion industry, the use of AI, ML and 3D technologies will bring much comfort to consumers. Indian textile and garment makers are also experimenting with various emerging technologies for manufacturing. However, the move towards finding the right fit for the Indian consumer is becoming a priority. Such projects have the potential to bring a wealth of consumer data for garment makers. While the sizing chart will be local, this will trigger a wider and continuing effort to create customized clothes and footwear for the Indian consumer. As a result, sharper focus on consumer needs can now be done at lower costs and help cater to the affordable market categories too.

## Deepfakes

At first glance the very concept of deepfake videos or voices appear criminal. Someone using deep learning AI to simulate the face and voice of a person cannot be considered acceptable or legal. Social media companies are struggling with various types of manipulated media that are often used to support fake information. However, a pioneering set of companies are using simulated videos and voices for genuine objectives. Much like ethical hackers who work for good, these companies have created digital avatars for various applications including public awareness campaigns and marketing initiatives apart from education and training.

Soccer legend David Beckham lent his voice for creating a public service message in nine different languages. AI was deployed to record an anti-malaria campaign in Beckham's voice even though he did not actually say all the words in the message in languages that he probably did not understand.

The US tech firm Synthesia, which developed the project with Beckham, has a wider set of AI offerings for training options. Companies can choose from over forty avatars created by Synthesia for online training. After selecting an avatar, a company can add data and content. Within a short time, a 'digital trainer' will be ready to deliver a training programme with realistic voice and video. Synthesia says that cameras, actors or actual trainers are not needed for creating videos.

While some companies are creating digital avatars with unique faces and voices, some other companies are using real-life personalities. People are renting their faces and images or allowing the usage for companies to create digital avatars.

The companies will pay a fee to people allowing the usage of their image to create marketing messages or training videos. A video of such a person can be used for various ads or promotions in different markets and languages.

Tel Aviv-based Hour One is performing leading edge-work with rented faces. Unlike a purely digital face, Hour One will record a few videos in high resolution with the person who has agreed to lend their image. Once it is recorded, AI will take over.

Any text in any language can be mouthed by a moving image created by AI.

The technology for creating avatars and deepfakes is similar. The key difference is legality, permissions and disclosures. Most deepfakes found online have illegally used faces and images of known personalities. Digital platforms are in a constant battle to remove such illegal and malicious content.

Legally approved deepfakes are the way ahead for the synthetic media industry. In the movie business, computer-generated images have been totally acceptable. For shooting dangerous action scenes, stunt doubles are used too. With strides in deepfake, movie producers can use AI to make characters perform tricks without risking anyone's safety. The younger version of the Star Wars character Princess Leia was created using similar technology.

Videos of historical characters or prominent personalities who are deceased can be created for educational purposes. Several experimental projects are being implemented in various sectors by various startups.

Digitally generated images, videos and voices can be used for many applications. Such efforts will require a strong set of guidelines if not regulation. At the centre of such guidelines should be disclosures to ensure that viewers are not misled. Viewers and consumers have a role to play by demanding disclosures and transparency from synthetic media creators. Approvals and permissions from individuals whose images are being used must also be a part of the process.

While the entertainment industry has been an early adopter, the deployment of synthetic images has the potential of making a deep impact on the advertising, marketing and training industry.

## Tech for Spying

In an era of voluntary data sharing, mobile phone tracking and cyber threats, spying has become relatively easy. Even so, new emerging technologies are helping corporates and governments in not just advanced intelligence gathering but also counter-measures to protect information.

Many governments are actively combining their national security concerns with their technological abilities. The US government's National Security Commission on Artificial Intelligence (NSCAI) is one such example. The NSCAI brought political leaders, technologists and security experts to chart the path for using technology for national security, intelligence gathering and building economic heft.

The chair of the commission was Eric Schmidt, former CEO of Google. Its members included Andy Jassy, CEO of Amazon, and former deputy secretary of defence, Robert Work. 'AI concepts and technologies for military and other malign uses and cheap and commercially available AI applications ranging from "deep fakes" to lethal drones become available to rogue states, terrorists, and criminals. The United States must prepare to defend against these threats by quickly and responsibly adopting AI for national security and defence purposes,' said the report of the commission released in 2021.[6]

Intelligence officers face an overload of information. Only data science can help intelligence agencies in sorting useful information from useless data. Add to this layers of pattern recognition and predictive analysis. 'The most immediate application of AI for processing is helping to "triage" and sort the intelligence community's massive data and information flows, automating tedious and time-intensive tasks still often done manually,' says an analytical brief by the Centre for Strategic and

International Studies. 'AI tools and analytics can also be exploited to enable human specialists in their core mission: identifying, recruiting and securing intelligence from foreign agents.'

The intelligence communities in most countries are working with the private sector to develop homegrown technology capabilities. A venture capital fund called In-Q-Tel works closely with the US intelligence agencies and invests in spy-tech companies. The company's aim is 'to invest in cutting-edge technologies to enhance the national security of the United States. IQT focuses on the 15,000+ early-stage venture-backed startup companies in the US and selects other countries. IQT also identifies and analyses technologies in all stages of development that are critical to national security.'

India is also warming up to collaborating with domestic technology companies to boost their intelligence and defence capabilities using emerging technologies. India is encouraging startups to work with defence organizations to create software as well as hardware like drones for defence and intelligence purposes.

Drone attacks, phone hacking, cybersecurity and hidden cameras get a lot of attention in popular culture and public discourse. However, the use of emerging technologies by intelligence communities will be much deeper than what is visible. High-level intelligence collection will no longer be the preserve of government agencies alone. For example, the increasing use of satellite visuals will require image analysis software created by startups. The pandemic era also brings to mind the need for counterintelligence on potential biowarfare. The Center for Strategic and International Studies paper 'Harnessing Emerging Technologies for Intelligence Collection' suggests that a new category of 'bio-intelligence' will rise rapidly.[7]

Emerging tech is being deployed by not just government agencies but also the corporate world to get market intelligence and information on competitors. This includes surveillance software development, video surveillance, big data, biometrics, domestic drones, face recognition technology, RFID chips and stingray tracking devices. Thus, surveillance and intelligence gathering have become more than just phone tapping.

## Summary

Sector-oriented innovation will continue to disrupt revenue models and investment priorities. Companies that are spending more on cybersecurity should now ensure that critical infrastructure is designed to withstand digital attacks. Nearly every industrial equipment carries information about it and is connected to other machines. This itself has ended the era of standalone machines chugging away in factory corners. The deployment of 5G, 6G and Wi-Fi 6 networks will bring even more systemic changes to business models. Safety and security will be an integral feature in each new technology solution.

# 7

# Firing Up Green Digital Energy

Anew experiment is taking place in East England. A London-based energy company, Centrica, will inject hydrogen gas into its natural gas plant as a 122-month experimental pilot project. The objective of the experiment is to see how hydrogen can reduce the carbon impact of natural gas. As per the company, 'Mixing hydrogen with natural gas reduces the overall carbon intensity.'

'This is the first time hydrogen will be used within a grid-connected gas-fired power plant in the UK, making this trial an important step forward towards realizing the role hydrogen can play in decarbonizing our energy system,' says Alexander Stafford, MP, chair of the Hydrogen All Party Parliamentary Group. This is an experimental step in bringing a new energy mix to power companies, underlining the ongoing disruptions in the energy sector.[1]

'There is huge investment riding on the future of clean energy infrastructure, with the US looking to invest 5 trillion dollars, as well as the European Union and the UK who have set clear-cut goals in terms of electrification goals, along with a £4 billion and a 10 point plan to be implemented by 2030,' says Aniket Patange, head of artificial intelligence and innovation at Hitachi.[2]

## The Energy Flash

As the world enhances its efforts to mitigate the impact of climate change, it will have to rely much on emerging technologies and energy sources. A report by WEF highlights that the transition to low-carbon energy can be accelerated and deepened only by the focused application of AI. The WEF in its report *Harnessing AI to Accelerate Energy Transition*[3] has identified the prominent transformations happening in the sector and underlined the critical role that emerging tech is playing in it.

Given the much-threatening conditions of global warming, the foundational energy transition from fossil to renewables needs to happen at scale and rapidly for any positive impact on the environment. However, it comes with its own set of challenges.

One of the fundamental issues in this transition is grid stability. The massive deployment of renewable energy sources demands a complete overhaul of the grid from how it has been operating traditionally. The grids, originally built for fossil fuel-based power generation, now have to deal with unpredictable and intermittent supply as renewable energy is not a steady source and relies on weather conditions and seasons; solar works on sunny days and wind turbines when there is a strong breeze.

Such intermittent supply not only makes it difficult for managers who must maintain the stability of energy passing through the grid but also puts tremendous stress on the grid itself. Another major reason for this intensified pressure on the grid is because of the time required for setting up renewable power generation, which is much less than that for setting up transmission and distribution lines.

To address these fast-paced transitions and to cope with the rising supply and integration of renewable energy, electricity grids now require better management to ensure higher efficiency levels.

The WEF report flags several cases that hurt a grid's stability, especially with intermittent power increase, which leads to challenges such as frequency imbalances, blackouts-brownouts and also significant capacity overbuilds. 'Without real-time data, advanced analytics and automation, the increasingly complex power and energy systems of the future will become impossible to manage,' the WEF says.

In this scenario, AI is poised to play a significant role in optimizing and even adding to the life cycle of existing grid infrastructure. With predictive analysis, AI can anticipate the amount of power that will reach the grid by combining weather conditions with supply parameters. This will allow grid managers to not only remain prepared but also deal with unanticipated surges in supply in an effective way. The report also adds, 'In the future, there will be vastly more physical assets connected to the power grid and, in particular, the distribution grid, where power flows will be increasingly dynamic and multidirectional.'

Research firm BloombergNEF (BNEF), which contributed to the report, noted that '13 per cent of all global power capacity in 2050 will comprise distributed small-scale photovoltaic (PV) energy and batteries, up from 4 per cent today. This will accelerate an ongoing trend of shrinking median power plant to shrink over 80 per cent.'

The rise of energy storage in batteries makes it possible to reuse power when required. It lends households the option of switching between battery power, on-site solar source and grid power based on their need. However, such switching at a large scale across millions of homes requires serious real-time tracking of usage to be able to manage grid load efficiently. AI-powered platforms are well-positioned to track and analyse this usage. Even for individuals, AI can help decide the charging of electric vehicles (EVs) by identifying a preferable time and duration based on peak or off-peak rates.

German Energy Agency, another contributor to the WEF report, says that AI can help in the efficient designing and location of solar, wind and other renewable farms. According to the report, 56 per cent of power generation could be provided by solar and wind in 2050—a massive 7.6 TW of solar and 4.6 TW of wind. And this would need a US$15.1 trillion investment in solar, wind and batteries, and a US$14 trillion power grid investment by 2050. According to BNEF, the power system costs would be higher by 6–13 per cent in 2040 if intelligent automation systems are not used.

There are four key shifts that are set to drive disruption of business models in the power and energy sector, according to MarketsandMarkets analysis. First is sustainability where green hydrogen, carbon capture and utilization will be critical. Second is energy storage where the form, shape and ease of usage will drive the market. Third is digital in energy where use of AI and

IoT as mentioned earlier will shift the dynamics. Fourth is smart transmission and distribution where demand and supply will be matched with precision.

Let us unpack each of these trends in the ensuing sections.

## Sustainability

### Green Hydrogen

Green hydrogen is among the cleanest fuels available in the market and has vast potential to decarbonize the existing energy system. It is a viable option and is best served by long-term investments by governments.

According to MarketsandMarkets estimates, the global green hydrogen market is projected to reach 1,723 kT by 2026, at a CAGR of 75 per cent while the market size for green hydrogen is expected to reach US$4.4 billion by 2026. This growth is attributed to the rising demand for green hydrogen from mobility, chemical, power generation, grid injection, industrials and other industries (CHP + domestic heat). Even globally, the market is expected to continue its growth with increasing opportunities from the automobile, transportation and industrial sectors. Increasing government support through favourable fiscal policies for green hydrogen, especially in the European countries, is further pushing the green hydrogen market, chiefly in the mobility end-use segment. Currently, the major countries for import–export are China, the US, Germany, the UK, France, and Japan, among others.

China is a growing market for green hydrogen. Along with production, it is also targeting nearly one million fuel cell-based vehicles by 2030. While China has massive potential for renewable energy, it aims to gain dominance in the hydrogen market too. The country is investing in a holistic hydrogen value chain to develop its sustainably.

The green hydrogen market has been largely dominated by alkaline electrolysis technology, which accounted for a 61.7 per cent share of the overall market, in terms of value, in 2020. This dominance is attributed to its key advantages over other manufacturing technologies. In comparison to polymer electrolyte membrane (PEM) electrolysis, alkaline electrolysis tends to produce highly pure green hydrogen. Considering these hydrogen ions do not diffuse easily into an electrolyte solution, they are highly preferred.

However, the market size for PEM electrolysis technology is also projected to reach US$1.9 billion by 2026, registering a promising CAGR of 61.5 per cent between 2021 and 2026. And, the global automotive fuel cell market is expected to account for a sale of 5,95,255 units in 2028, growing at a CAGR of 62.2 per cent during the forecast period. Europe is the major market for both alkaline electrolysis and PEM electrolysis technologies in the green hydrogen market.

From a usage standpoint, mobility is the largest end-use industry of the green hydrogen market and the fastest growing sector at a CAGR of 61.3 per cent between 2021 and 2026. The increasing use of green hydrogen in fuel cell EVs is among the major reasons for market growth. Green hydrogen in the fuel cells of vehicles is a rapidly developing market as it offers the convenience of fossil fuels without the entailed emissions.

Power is expected to be the second fastest growing industry, showing nearly 60 per cent CAGR between 2021 and 2026 in terms of value. The high demand for green hydrogen also comes from the steel and chemical industries for decarburization.

Green hydrogen has developed multiple applications compared to its general image of fuel cells in electric cars. It is now used to make alternative fuels, also known as energy carriers, such as ammonia, methanol and synthetic liquids. These energy carriers show the potential to grow future demand and acceptance in countries among leadership and industries that plan to have a low-carbon future. It can prove to be a no-carbon fuel for marine transportation and also a backup power in industries. This wide range of applications makes the venture of green hydrogen lucrative and shows potential to grow in the times to come.

Produced from green hydrogen using renewable sources of energy, green ammonia is the cleaner version of ammonia gas. Hydrogen and green ammonia are likely to become the future fuel for the transportation and maritime industries as they are under immense pressure to cut down their emission level. This, along with the fast-expanding hydrogen-based economy, is bringing immense opportunities in the green ammonia market. The shipping industry accounts for 3 per cent of the global greenhouse emissions. This is mainly due to the high consumption of diesel and high-sulphur fuel by ships. The maritime industry is obliged to cut down its emission by using cleaner fuels and, hence, is undergoing major transformations. Ammonia is the highest carrier of hydrogen, which is high energy density and can provide energy to ships and reduce the emissions simultaneously.

The fertilizer industry is another major consumer of green ammonia. Of the overall ammonia produced, approximately 90 per cent is consumed by the fertilizer sector. With manufacturers now focusing on reducing their dependence on fossil fuels, the emergence of advanced electrolysis technologies for enhancing the fertilizer production process and ensuring energy efficiency is gaining momentum and subsequently expanding the green ammonia market.

## Carbon Capture and Its Utilization

Another powerful emissions reduction technology that can be applied across varied energy systems is carbon capture, utilization and storage (or CCUS). The technology mainly collaborates with energy guzzlers like oil and gas plants and coal plants in pre- or post-combustion stages to store $CO_2$. The $CO_2$ generated in these plants is stored in underground storage tanks and is to be recycled into usable fuel. Among $CO_2$ mitigation options, CCUS is regarded as the technology that can significantly reduce the emissions of $CO_2$ from fossil fuel combustion sources. For example, a plant in Iceland is producing methanol from captured and recycled carbon.[4] The technology is currently at the nascent stage of development but has the potential to change the landscape of traditional energy production shifts to renewable energy production.

The CCUS is a three-stage process: capture, transport and storage.

$CO_2$, once captured from the power plants or industrial facilities, is transported to storage sites through ships, pipelines or trucks. The CCUS process can capture up to 95 per cent of $CO_2$ emissions from a plant that can be utilized for enhanced oil/gas recovery or various commodities, including dry ice, urea and carbonated beverages.

The CCUS market is expected to grow rapidly due to the growing need for mitigating carbon emissions and achieving a greener and healthier environment. The oil and gas end-use industry is the largest segment of the CCUS market. The increasing focus of governments of several countries, including the US, Canada, the UK and Australia, is promoting CCUS by offering tax credits and other benefits to fuel the market. Some early signs of the adoption of CCUS can be seen as Elon Musk has launched a US$100 million competition to find the best carbon capture technologies. The UK government has also included CCUS in its green ten-point plan highlighting its goal to have at least one power CCUS project operational by 2030.

## Energy Storage

A battery energy storage system (BESS) comprises an energy storage medium and other ancillary equipment to protect and control the system. It is primarily used to reduce peak demand charges, integrate renewable sources, regulate voltage and frequency and provide a backup power supply. Various advancements have taken place based on battery types. The BESS market has been classified into lithium-ion batteries, advanced lead-acid batteries, flow batteries, other batteries, which include sodium-based batteries, nickel–cadmium batteries, nickel–metal hydride, nickel–iron batteries and flywheel batteries.

The BESS market was valued at US$3.5 billion in 2021 and is projected to reach US$15,134.2 billion by 2027, growing at a CAGR of 27.9 per cent between 2022 and 2027. This growth is attributed to the increasing demand for grid energy storage systems as a result of the ongoing grid modernization and growing penetration of lithium-ion batteries in the renewable energy sector. It is also owing to the move towards adopting a low-carbon and less fossil fuel-based economy and the ongoing renewable energy revolution. BESS are highly adopted for utility and commercial operations as they ensure the availability of power when customers need it the most. The ecosystem of BESS can generate new revenue capabilities with the introduction of batteries compatible with smart factories and the industrial IoT devices, and the introduction of liquid metal batteries.

A few of the future battery technologies that are expected to boost the battery market over the forecast period include sodium sulphur battery, cobalt-free battery, metal air battery and many more. Companies are heavily investing in research and development activities to produce improved batteries. The prime reason behind the adoption of batteries is the benefits provided by them. Lithium-ion, lead-acid and flow batteries are among the highly adopted batteries in commercial, residential and utility applications. Lithium-ion batteries are one of the most efficient energy storage devices used worldwide. Recent developments and claims made by lithium-ion battery manufacturers and automobile companies suggest that the prices of these batteries are expected to decline substantially in the coming years. The on-grid connection segment held a larger size of the BESS market in 2021. The market for on-grid connection is projected to reach US$12.9 billion by 2027, growing at a higher CAGR of 28.2 per cent between 2022 and 2027.

Similarly, thermal energy storage (TES) is a technology that stores thermal energy by either heating or cooling a storage medium. Thermal energy is stored to be used later for heating and cooling applications and also for power generation. TES systems are used particularly in building and industrial processes. This energy storage system consists of three components: the storage medium, a heat transfer mechanism and the containment system. The storage medium has thermal energy either in the form of sensible heat, latent heat of the phase change medium (PCM) or in the form of reversible chemical reaction [thermochemical storage (TCS)] of the substance to the surface of another solid or liquid. The market for TES is estimated to grow by US$369 million by 2025 at a CAGR of 14.4 per cent.

## Digital in Energy

The energy sector has been one of the early adopters of digital technologies. In the 1970s, power utilities were known as the digital pioneers as they embraced the latest technologies to support grid operation and management. Over the last few years, digitization in the energy sector has continued apace ensuring grid stability, improving efficiency, saving costs and reducing losses. In today's scenario, with rising climate concerns and the unprecedented need to move towards cleaner sources of energy generation, the adoption of innovative technologies has become ever more critical. It is set to play a crucial role as an enabler of sustainable development and climate resilience. Major energy demand segments such as oil and gas, transport, buildings, large industries and data centres are navigating through major shifts in their business models and consistently exploring the transformational potential of digitalization to improve operations.

According to a report by McKinsey, energy companies that have applied digitization successfully have witnessed 2 per cent to 10 per cent improvements in production and are yielding 10 per cent to 30 per cent improvements in cost.[5]

## Digitalization in Industries Accounting for Highest Energy Consumption

Technology has already made significant strides in sectors that demand the highest levels of energy and power. These industries include utility, transport, oil and gas, and buildings.

Transport accounts for around 28 per cent of the global final energy demand and 23 per cent of global $CO_2$ emissions from fuel combustion.[6] By deploying newer technologies and solutions, the industry is rapidly shifting towards a highly data-driven approach in a bid to combat energy demand and usage. In transportation, digital platforms, such as MaaS, are now among the fastest-growing business models to further enable and boost energy efficiency. A report by Deloitte on the rise of MaaS explains how people in Finland's capital, Helsinki, are using a popular app called Whim to plan their journey. Interestingly, Helsinki aims to make it unnecessary for any city resident to own a private car by 2025.[7] The innovation aims to reduce carbon emissions by reducing the number of cars on the road and optimizing travelling for commuters.

For buildings, it is energy as a service (EaaS) that is attracting a large number of early-stage venture investments to innovative and new business models. Commercial and industrial customers are increasingly opting for pay-for-performance contracts with EaaS companies in order to retrofit their premises to ensure the optimization of energy usage and loss reduction.

In the oil and gas sector, a MarketsandMarkets report estimates that the value of AI was about US$2.85 billion in 2022 and was set to grow further. It is also estimated that the oil-focused digital services sector will increase from US$5 billion as on 2022 to over US$30 billion annually by 2025, contributing US$150 billion in annual savings for oil companies. Machine learning, AI, the IoT and blockchain are steadily becoming the defining features of these industries.

## Major Technologies Defining the Energy Landscape

The IoT in the energy market has been growing rapidly as it aims to enhance operational effectiveness, provide analytics-based decisions and improve production. The IoT in energy offers upgraded security and proper management of assets.

Energy is and will always remain one of the crucial resources for any country. And monitoring energy usage across will always be an overwhelming task, with excess data, in the absence of proper technology interventions. IoT-based solutions have eventually reinforced competitive benefits and uncovered new business prospects. Improved supply chain, enhanced asset monitoring and maintenance and potential return on IoT investment are some of the benefits that have already impacted the global energy industry.

The global IoT in energy market analysis consists of components (solutions, platform and services), applications and regions. The deployment of IoT-based smart energy solutions will result in better field communication, reduced cost of maintenance, real-time monitoring, digital oil field infrastructure, reduced power consumption, mine automation, greater safety and security of assets and, thus, higher productivity.

The IoT in the energy market is expected to grow US$35.2 billion by 2025. Along with IoT, blockchain technology in the energy sector is also getting acceptance consistently. By making electricity a tradable asset on a blockchain, consumers can benefit from the many advantages of blockchain commerce such as variable electricity rates, energy payments, peer-to-peer energy trading, low transaction costs and network transparency.

Some blockchain-based enterprises across the globe have started adopting the technology to improve the transparency and efficiency in operations and enhance the overall experience for energy-delivery services. Therefore, the increasing popularity of blockchain technology in the government sector is expected to be one of the major market drivers.

The global blockchain market is expected to be worth US$67.3 billion by 2026 and in the energy segment, the market is projected to reach US$7.11 billion by 2023. The factors driving the market include growing interest in blockchain technology, rising adoption in the energy sector, utilizing blockchain technology to create transparent and efficient transactions, increasing instances of fraudulent activities and the growing need to protect data from tampering.

## Smart Transmission and Distribution

Technological advancements are fundamentally reshaping and transforming the electrical grid infrastructure. The grids are becoming smarter with the integration of the IoT, cloud, analytics and smart devices. A smart grid unifies ICT (information and communication technology) along the entire value chain of electric utility, from generation to transmission and distribution. The utilities are consistently shifting their focus towards cutting-edge technologies to optimize efficiency and increase profitability without losing sight of long-term goals.

Upgradation and modernization of the expanding electricity transmission and distribution infrastructure, restricting electricity theft and the interconnection of the existing grids with the new ones are boosting the growth of the market. The endeavours of government bodies of both developed and developing economies to provide accurate electricity consumption recording and an efficient data management system have led them to heavily invest in the T&D infrastructure. This is further acting as a catalyst for the smart electric metre market.

According to an estimate, China along with India in the Asia–Pacific region has spent over US$1.5 trillion on construction activities in 2013. China is a relatively low-cost manufacturing base, which proves to be an attractive market for global smart electric manufacturers for sale to the domestic market and for export.

## Microgrids

The microgrid market is estimated to grow from US$24.6 billion in 2021 to US$42.3 billion by 2026 at a CAGR of 11.4 per cent during 2021–26. This growth is largely driven by factors such as rising focus on decarbonization by various end users and government, increase in demand for uninterrupted power supply, efforts towards rural electrification and rising instances of cyberattacks on energy infrastructures. Initiatives by governments of different countries to encourage the development of microgrids are further fuelling the growth of the market.

In October 2019, the Federal Government of Australia launched a US$50 million microgrid funding programme for the country. Of this, US$20 million funding was allocated for microgrid feasibility studies in Australia as a part of the first round of the Regional and Remote Communities Reliability Fund of the Federal Government. Twelve energy generation-related projects in Canada received approximately US$10 million funding from the Ontario Smart Grid Fund in February 2018.

The decentralization of the electricity sector and making production sources closer to the place of consumption, supported with smart techniques, ensures reduction in losses and stability within the transmission network. One such example is of energy usage in buildings. According to IEA's Central Scenario, electricity used in buildings is set to nearly double from 11 petawatt hours (PWh) as of 2014 to around 20 PWh by 2040, resulting in a huge increase in demand for power-generation and network capacity. With technology innovations such as lighting sensors, auto-programme heating–cooling services, especially smart grids and energy storage, buildings are now intelligent buildings that are making a notable progress in achieving energy efficiency. These advancements are assisting building managers, network operators and other stakeholders with predictive maintenance and operational efficiency with real-time data.

Singapore's decarbonization strategy in its Green Plan for 2030 has an ambitious goal to quadruple solar energy deployment by 2025 and achieve 2 GWp (GigaWatts peak) of solar energy by 2030. From 2030, 80 per cent of new buildings will be 'super low energy' buildings with an 80 per cent improvement in energy efficiency compared to the 2005 consumption levels for best-in-class green buildings. At least 20 per cent of schools will be carbon neutral by 2030. In the near future, intelligent building energy management systems are expected to not only receive and store power from electricity generated onsite but also share excess electricity with a neighbourhood microgrid when able, or draw from these sources as needed.[8]

Commitment to net zero buildings is the primary driver towards the adoption of digitization in the sector. Smart equipment and appliances not only manage energy consumption and reduce emissions but also improve reliability and remote management. A 2021 study suggests that grid-interactive efficient buildings (GEBs) can reduce energy costs by up to 20 per cent through active demand management.[9]

As mentioned earlier in the chapter, renewable energy sources are growing exponentially and expected to account for nearly 70 per cent of global electricity production in 2050. Adapting to this increase in demand for renewable sources, grid reliability has become a primary concern.[10] The need of the hour is to make grids more flexible and resilient to deliver reliable power that is sustainable and affordable. Also, in the coming times, utilities are going to face a new set of competition, with oil majors significantly investing in renewables and storage.

Furthermore, the proliferation of electric vehicles is set to create huge pressure on grids. The number of electric vehicles is expected to grow from 5 million to 125 million in 2030. In such a scenario, the vehicle-to-grid technologies can be used to help manage grid peak loads, making it more resilient and helping meet aggressive renewable-energy goals. There are emerging tech startups in the smart cities space such as Ampcontrol, Bovlabs and Electric Fish that are working towards optimizing EV charging patterns while stabilizing grid load.

For example, Bovlabs had its first project deployed with SNCF train stations (one of the largest train stations in the world).[11] The idea was to charge the cars when they were parked at the station. Here, a commuter is offered to park free and needs to tell the system the return time. With the information, Bovlabs initiates the process of optimizing and tracking down the best possible profile to charge the vehicle.

## Summary

As climate change remains a serious concern, power companies are being pushed to reimagine their business models to cut energy wastage and also move towards alternative electric sources. Other major innovations in the sector include AI-powered smart grids to forecast energy demand, predict equipment breakdown and outages, facilitate smart asset management, improve efficiency and reduce wastage; self-piloted drones to keep track of facilities by capturing sensor data and high-quality images of equipment from various angles, and leverage sensor and video data for decision making; and the rise of prosumers as an outcome of the price fall in renewable energy technologies, where new market models such as peer-to peer, prosumer-to-grid, organized prosumer groups are seeing all-time high.

Technology innovation and creating new business models will remain at the core of the utilities' energy transition endeavours in the fifth industrial revolution. The current size of power generation stands at about 8,200 GW and is expected to reach approximately 12,000 GW by 2030, while the global transmission and distribution network will increase from approximately 80 million kms in 2021 to about 95 million kms by 2035, according to MarketsandMarkets, warranting an investment of more than $300 billion per year. Most of the generation capacity is based on fossil fuels, contributing around 60 per cent of the total generation capacity.

This market is changing and the business models based on fossil fuels usage are declining. Rising instead is the digital T&D market which stands at $45 billion per year, and battery storage which is expected to grow from approximately $4.4 billion in 2022 to $15 billion in 2030, and usage model.

The power of change is coursing through the electricity lines of the energy sector.

# 8

## High-Tech Healthcare

Prevention is better than cure and prediction helps prevention. New technologies are allowing healthcare providers to know more about patients even before a formal diagnosis is done. Consider this: sensors and devices can assess the internal body functions of a patient and alert doctors before the ailment worsens. Technological systems and insurance companies are proving services to patients to constantly monitor their health. From wearables to remote monitoring of patients, digital systems are helping predict and prevent ailments.

Decades ago, a doctor would use experience and instinct more than devices and instruments. Today a doctor is incomplete without high-tech machines and instruments. Tomorrow, the doctor will be a device.

Technology is offering new models that few would have anticipated. Several technological and ecosystem changes are occurring, which are driving deep shifts in healthcare. This is changing business models and structures in the healthcare sector across all its functions. Intensive healthcare can be made available at home and is no longer restricted to hospitals. Machines and medical teams are already shoulder-to-shoulder in operating rooms. Gene-based innovations are creating solutions at a nano level. AI is diagnosing and reading patterns at a speed and scale that is accelerating the efforts of scientific research.

Owing to the COVID-19 pandemic, the healthcare segment has seen an exponential rate of innovation and adoption of technologies in a short span of two years. In a survey conducted by Accenture, one out of four participants accepted that their access to healthcare has become better since the onset of the COVID-19 pandemic.[1] Empowered by digital technologies, healthcare consumers now expect medical services on demand, anytime and anywhere, further pushing the providers to develop new models of care in the emerging consumer-to-business (C2B) healthcare marketplace.

A series of innovative care-delivery business models are rapidly broadening the digital healthcare landscape. For example, the US is witnessing a rise in retail-based healthcare hubs. According to Gurpreet Singh, US health services leader for consulting firm PwC, 'The pandemic has driven growth in retail clinic usage.' A pre-pandemic 2019 survey by PwC's Health Research Institute found that 30 per cent of US adults had visited a retail clinic, while in September 2020, the share of respondents who visited a retail clinic had climbed to 40 per cent. The report noted that about three-quarters of respondents agreed they would use a retail clinic again.[2] In addition to this, telemedicine or telehealth can be called the new normal due to preference as well as necessity.

The shift towards digital healthcare is expected to change the patient–provider relationship forever. With deep learning algorithms reading CT scans faster than humans to natural language processing (NLP) combing through and analysing unstructured data in electronic health records (EHRs), several reports indicate how new technologies, especially AI, can even take over a doctor's role completely, although it remains highly debatable. As per experts, the natural settling point in the industry would be a blend of human experience and digital augmentation.

On the consumer side, the C2B platforms are empowering users to create their own customized-to-me systems of care and thus threatening the value proposition of today's proprietary networks. Consumers can select services based on quality, cost and convenience, guided by AI and machine learning (ML) agents. This is also leading to more market-driven pricing for medical services. The platforms and C2B models are propagating more transparency, accelerating positive transformations in terms of healthcare for all, eliminating opaque pricing and generating quality data that had initially slowed the industry disruption.[3]

## Technology Adoption in the Segment

According to a Cognizant report, social, mobile, analytics and cloud (SMAC) have been the four key disruptors of the healthcare industry.[4] Today, these form the baseline of a digital healthcare system, which is getting further complimented by newer technologies such as AI, 5G, IoT, virtual reality (VR) and AR, blockchain and other next-generation computing techniques. Hospitals are becoming smarter with AI, the internet of medical things (IoMT) and data management practices. These solutions are not only enhancing workflows but also improving staff scheduling with the use of connected infrastructure, and devices and systems that ensure accurate and equitable clinical services. Utilizing the data generated, providers are leveraging predictive analytics for better decision-making, improving patient outcomes and, most importantly, providing relief to healthcare workers. According to an analysis by McKinsey, the use of telehealth increased thirty-eight-fold from the pre-COVID-19 baseline.[5] Many healthcare organizations are creating new models of soft launches which can receive consumer feedback before final release. Moreover, unprecedented levels of collaboration have been witnessed between 2020 and 2022. For example, as healthcare and auto industries teamed up to build ventilators, healthcare providers also partnered with technology companies to deliver COVID-19 apps and solutions.

During the COVID-19 pandemic period, the world also witnessed the establishment of virtual hospital wards to reduce the load on hospital infrastructure and keep beds free for more critical patients. These wards are equipped with centralized communication infrastructure and could oversee the treatment of numerous patients, all in their homes. This is now being advanced to virtual ER, a pilot project under development at the Pennsylvania Center for Emergency Medicine.[6] The programme will differentiate between a teleconsult, which is taking place already, and a televisit, which would begin under the pilot programme.[7]

Furthermore, medical robots such as microbots, nursing robots and sanitation robots are redefining healthcare like never before. Nursing robots are capable of taking up an immense amount of workload from the nurses, especially when the cases are very high. These robots can autonomously monitor patient vitals and also help with the lifting and transferring of patients. On the other hand, microbots are microscopic robots that can seamlessly travel through human bodies and even perform surgeries. Instead of cutting open a patient for an operation, microbots do it from the inside.

In a nutshell, the healthcare sector is witnessing prominent digital innovations covering research and development (R&D), wellness and disease prevention, screening and diagnosis, care delivery and finance and operations. These innovations can be largely categorized into four major sections: mobile health technology, health information technology, wearable technology and telehealth technology.

## Understanding Key Shifts

For most consumers and patients, the use of artificial intelligence in imaging is the first exposure to emerging technology in healthcare.

## Diagnostic Imaging

This field itself has several sub-sectors that are changing the way imaging is done. New models are appearing in teleradiology and multimodal imaging.

The application of AI in medical imaging and diagnostics is growing rapidly owing to several factors such as government initiatives to increase the adoption of AI-based technologies, increasing demand for AI tools in the imaging field, the influx of large and complex big data sets, growing focus on reducing the workload of radiologists and growth in funding of AI-based startups. However, the lack of a skilled AI workforce, ambiguity in regulations and reluctance among radiologists/practitioners to adopt these solutions remain major restraining factors.

## Creation of Large and Complex Data Sets

With the increasing digitization and adoption of information systems in the healthcare industry, big data (large and complex data) is generated at various stages of the care delivery process. In the medical diagnostics industry, big data comprises information generated from clickstream and web and social media interactions; readings from medical devices, such as sensors, ECGs, X-rays, healthcare claims and billing records and biometric data among other sources. Big data and analytical solutions have grown exponentially in sophistication and adoption in the last decade with the growing acceptance of EHRs, digitized laboratory slides and high-resolution radiology images among healthcare providers.

Currently, healthcare is one of the top five big data industries, especially in the US. In the coming years, the volume of big data in medical diagnostics is expected to increase as a result of the use of bidirectional patient portals that allow patients to upload their data and images to their EHRs.

After the implementation of legislation such as the Health Information Technology for Economic and Clinical Health (HITECH) Act in 2009 in the US, there has been a marked increase in the use of EHRs among healthcare providers. This can be attributed to the fact that under the HITECH Act, healthcare providers who use EHRs to advance clinical processes and improve outcomes are incentivized, while those who do not adhere to these requirements are penalized.

The need to efficiently manage the ever-increasing volume of large and complex medical diagnostic data is compelling the healthcare industry to turn its focus towards various AI-based solutions.

Radiologists are using AI-based solutions to shift their focus from interpreting images to providing better care. According to a study conducted by the Association of American Medical Colleges, in the US, the shortage of radiologists could increase to nearly 42,000 by 2033. At present, the country has as few as 100 radiologists per million population. As a result, radiologists are experiencing tremendous pressure and workload for the interpretation of endless diagnostic data, which is creating an opportunity for them to adopt AI solutions.

Currently, the US holds the largest share of AI in the medical diagnostics market in North America and is expected to exhibit high growth during the forecast period. Improvements in cloud computing platforms, which are now more efficient, affordable and capable of processing complex information, have led to the growth of inexpensive software development tools and vast data sets that play a vital role in the development of AI technology. China, Japan and India are among the major countries driving its growth in the medical diagnostics market in the Asia–Pacific region.

In 2020, the services segment accounted for the largest share—61.8 per cent—of AI in the medical diagnostics market globally. This segment is projected to reach US\$2.24 billion by 2025 at a CAGR of 48.7 per cent. The growth in the services segment can be attributed to the recurring requirements of technical services. The software segment is estimated to grow at the highest CAGR of 52.5 per cent during the forecast period.

Emerging markets such as India, China and Brazil are expected to offer significant growth opportunities for players operating AI in the medical diagnostics market. This can majorly be attributed to the rising patient population in these countries.

According to the National Institute of Health and Family Welfare (NIHFW), in India, it is estimated that there are 2 to 2.5 million cancer patients at any given point in time and every year about 0.7 million new cases are reported in the country. Furthermore, the healthcare sector in India and China is rapidly growing and resulting in the introduction of new medical technologies with a special focus on advanced imaging equipment. All these factors, coupled with the growing population, are expected to increase the medical imaging data volumes in their respective healthcare systems. This provides a great untapped development opportunity for AI-based solutions in emerging countries.

## Multimodal Imaging

The increasing demand for the early-stage diagnosis of any disease condition using multimodal imaging technologies, along with their growing applications, is a major factor driving market growth. The availability of funding for research as well as technological advancements in the field of multimodal imaging—especially in nuclear medicine—has led to significant growth in its market space. For example, scientists Simon Cherry and Ramsey Badawi at the University of California, Davis (US) conceptualized a total-body scanner in 2005. Their project attracted US$1.5 million in funding from the US National Cancer Institute in 2011 and US$15.5 million from the US NIH in 2015, and the scientists eventually collaborated with United Imaging Healthcare to develop the uEXPLORER PET/CT system.

## Teleradiology

Teleradiology enables the transmission of diagnostic medical images from one location to another, where radiologists and physicians can access them. It enables radiologists to provide their expertise without necessarily being at the same location as the patient. Many super-specialist radiologists are typically located in metropolitan cities. The adoption of teleradiology solutions has significantly helped bridge the rural–urban disparity in many emerging countries and developed economies. These solutions are more convenient and cost-effective as they eliminate the need for travel and allow radiologists to work from anywhere.

A breakthrough expected in the teleradiology domain is the advent of 3D report viewing, as the deployment and utilization of sophisticated CT and MRI 3D imaging services increase data complexity. Consequently, there is a rising need to incorporate efficient assimilation solutions to streamline workflow. A key obstacle physicians face is storing patient data, which often involves copious amounts of paperwork. Key players such as Philips Healthcare (Netherlands), Teleradiology Solutions (Telradsol) (US), USARDA Holdings (US) and Medica Group (UK) offer highly specialized report-viewing services.

The increasing use of cloud-based solutions in healthcare facilities is expected to impact the market for teleradiology positively as they require less investment for static IT architecture and help overcome geographical barriers. In addition, the ability to store and share images on a cloud-based system is essential for maximizing efficiencies.

The rise in imaging procedures is expected to drive the demand for advanced teleradiology solutions for reliability and efficiency. According to an article published in July 2020 by the University College London, in the National Health Service in the UK, about five million CT scans are performed every year; in the US, it is more than eighty million annually, which accounts for a quarter of Americans' total exposure to radiation. A high degree of technical skill and expertise is required to handle advanced and sophisticated diagnostic imaging systems, thus fuelling the growing complexity of cases with a shortage of adequate resources.

Consequently, physical fatigue arising from putting in extra work hours to enhance efficiency is rising and hence frequent episodes of radiologist burnout experiences. Teleradiology is an effective approach to combat this escalating fatigue rate.

## Genomics and Next-Generation Sequencing

The discovery of new biomarkers for various diseases, especially cancer, has brought about revolutionary changes in the field of medical diagnostics. Continuous developments in sequencing technologies and a better understanding of genomics have increased the efficiency of biomarkers in disease detection. As precise diagnosis and personalized medicine increase survival rate as well as reduce the financial burden on national health insurance programmes, governments across the globe are expected to make significant investments in genome sciences, which will ensure a positive future demand for next-generation sequencing (NGS) in such applications.

Advancements in NGS technologies are further transforming the landscape through reduced costs of sequencing platforms and systems as well as the sequencing process itself. The regulatory and reimbursement outlook for NGS has improved considerably in recent years, which also serves to boost the adoption of sequencing technologies among a wider user base. Many institutes prefer NGS systems that have overridden microarray technology. The applications of NGS in cancer treatment and precision medicine are also generating widespread interest. As prices are expected to decrease further in the coming years, NGS-based tests are expected to be considered under healthcare insurance policies for reimbursement.

MarketsandMarkets has identified a revenue opportunity worth US$21.4 billion in the adjacent markets of NGS over the next five years; these are data storage and management, high-performance computing (HPC), AI in genomics and lab automation. Data analysis, storage and management contribute over 67 per cent of the opportunity pocket. NGS data analysis methods are revolutionizing the drug discovery and development areas through predictive analytics, ML and big data analytics.

The quantity of data produced during whole-genome sequencing is usually in the range of terabytes, which makes its management a major concern in NGS sequencing. Storage requirements can be complex due to inconsistencies in formats and the lack of industry-wide standardization for output, which reflects a massive opportunity for data management and security in this market.

However, the application of big data technologies and AI for NGS analysis, as well as the management of workflows, has significantly increased the yield of NGS runs.

The growing incidence of cancer and increasing applications of NGS in therapeutic research are some of the strongest drivers of this change. Cancer is among the leading causes of death worldwide. Increasing lifestyle changes, high levels of industrial and environmental pollution and the inadvertent entry of chemicals into the human food chain are factors that are causing an alarming rise in cancer incidence. The combination of NGS and advanced computational data analysis approaches have revolutionized the understanding of the genomic underpinnings of cancer development and progression.

According to MarketsandMarkets estimates, the NGS market is projected to reach US$424.2 billion by 2026 from US$10.2 billion in 2021, at a CAGR of 18.7 per cent. Market growth is largely driven by the advancements in NGS platforms, declining costs of genome sequencing, improving regulatory and reimbursement scenarios for NGS-based diagnostic tests, and the growing incidence of cancer and the increasing applications of NGS in cancer research. The NGS market in Asia–Pacific is projected to register the highest CAGR of 21.7 per cent by 2026. The increasing financial support from the public and private agencies, increasing number of NGS-based research projects, growing awareness about precision medicine and the high incidence of chronic diseases are some of the key factors driving the growth of the Asia–Pacific NGS market.

## Gene Editing

One of the most powerful tools that has emerged as thin gene editing technology is clustered regularly interspaced short palindromic repeats (CRISPR). Scientists are hopeful of not just treating but also cutting off the genes responsible for therapeutic indications including oncology and neurodegenerative diseases. CRISPR-Cas9 is a revolutionary genome-editing technique that facilitates the efficient and directed alterations of the eukaryotic genome. It also enables the introduction of insertion or deletion mutations, the deletion of large genomic loci and the introduction of specific small DNA changes.

Genomics has several application areas, including the identification of human genetic disorders, drug discovery, agriculture, veterinary sciences and forensics. The application of genomics in forensic studies has increased significantly with the advent of NGS, particularly due to the products offered by Illumina (US) specifically designed for forensic science. Earlier, DNA analysis was used for fingerprint profiling, whereas currently NGS helps in the analysis of a specimen at the scene of a crime and enables the extraction of greater amounts of information from a trace or a damaged DNA sample. As genome editing is critical in the analysis and profiling of DNA, RNA, mtDNA and other genetic material obtained from plants and animals, the expanding applications of genomics will create a proportionate demand for gene editing methods. The genome editing/genome engineering market is projected to reach US$11.7 billion by 2026 from US$5.1 billion in 2021, at a CAGR of 18.2 per cent during the forecast period.

## AI in Genomics

Precision medicine remains one of the most transformational and revolutionary applications in the healthcare sector. Integration of AI in genomics has enabled its faster and more efficient application. Autoimmune diseases, infectious diseases and cancer have become increasingly difficult to treat using conventional methods that do not consider individual genetic, environmental and lifestyle differences. In this application, precision medicine software helps researchers and medical practitioners cure people and empowers individuals to monitor and take a more active role in their health. While AI implementation in medical care and management is still in its early stages, it showcases high potential by seamlessly integrating large-scale patient data.

Manual methods are becoming increasingly dispensable as the use of automation in genomics as high-throughput requirements are on the rise due to greater reproducibility and throughput as compared to manual methods.

AI algorithms are used to create synthetic patient populations with the properties of actual patient cohorts and build personalized and predictive models of drug combinations. They reveal complex relationships between diets, microbiomes and genetic line-ups to determine the comparative treatment response. AI-inspired ML methods leverage the volume and exponential growth of genomic data to translate genetic information into new unforeseen insights for safer, more effective and cost-efficient personalized healthcare. Thus, the ability of AI to seamlessly integrate patient data and provide actionable insights can revolutionize precision medicine.

The AI in the genomics market is projected to reach US$1.7 billion by 2025, from US$201.5 million in 2020, at a CAGR of 52.7 per cent. The need to control drug development and discovery costs and time, increasing public and private investments in AI in genomics and the adoption of AI solutions in precision medicine are driving the growth of this market. However, the lack of a skilled AI workforce and ambiguous regulatory guidelines for medical software are expected to restrain the market growth during the forecast period.

## Advanced Therapy Medicinal Products

Advanced therapy medicinal products (ATMPs) are medicines and therapeutic treatments that include gene therapy medicinal products, somatic cell therapy medicinal products and tissue-engineered products. They offer cutting-edge innovation and major hope for various diseases for which there are limited or no therapeutic options.

## Gene Therapy Medicines

These contain genes that lead to a therapeutic, prophylactic or diagnostic effect. They work by inserting 'recombinant' genes into the body, usually to treat a variety of diseases, including genetic disorders, cancer or long-term diseases. In vivo viral vector-based therapy (Zolgensma, Luxturna), plasmid-based therapy (Neovasculagen, HGF Plasmid) and RNA-based therapy (Onpattro, Givlaari) are some examples of gene therapy medicines.

## Cell Therapy Medicines

These contain cells or tissues that have been manipulated to change their biological characteristics or cells or tissues not intended to be used for the same essential functions in the body. They can be used to cure, diagnose or prevent diseases. This category includes all types of cell therapy, excluding stem cell therapy. T-Cell therapy (Kymriah, Yescarta and Zalmoxis) and dendritic cell therapy (Provenge and Immuncell-LC) are some examples.

## Tissue-Engineered Medicines

These contain cells or tissues that have been modified so that they can be used to repair, regenerate or replace human tissue. Regenerative medicine refers to methods to replace or regenerate human cells, tissues or organs in order to restore or establish normal function. This includes cell therapies, tissue engineering, gene therapy and biomedical engineering techniques, as well as more traditional treatments involving pharmaceuticals, biologics and devices.

Currently, more than a thousand cell and gene therapies are in the various phases of clinical trials worldwide. In the US alone, there are more than seven hundred investigational cell and gene therapies in clinical development. However, manufacturing facilities have not kept up. It has been estimated that hundreds of facilities will be needed to manufacture the treatments that are now in clinical trials. One of the areas that needs to be accelerated is viral capacity. Most viral vectors are produced using adherent manufacturing, which is expensive to operate. For example, a vial of twenty million cells can cost US$20,000 to US$30,000 to make. The cost of manufacturing a gene therapy can be between US$500,000 and US$1 million, excluding the cost for research and development, the cost to run crucial clinical trials or the cost to build the commercial infrastructure necessary to provide access to patients.

Due to the complexity of both the cells (product) and treatment logistics, relatively low production volumes and the large number of manual manipulations involved with current methods, cell therapies are expensive to produce. The manufacturing costs of cell therapy treatments are estimated to be more than US$100,000 per patient. Thus, the affordability of cell therapy products will be an important issue and challenge for both manufacturers and healthcare providers.

The global cell and gene therapy market (excluding oligonucleotides) is estimated to reach US$21.3 billion by 2027 from US$3.1 billion in 2020. The increasing incidence of cancer and neurological diseases is a major factor supporting this market growth

Due to the high level of personalization required during the development of autologous therapies, the cost of delivering them to patients is extremely high. Therefore, such therapies are referred to as following a service-based model. With insurance and healthcare systems consistently striving to reduce costs, such a model is unattractive, and cheaper traditional treatments are preferred.

Multiple companies are continuously striving to achieve efficacious production processes, increasing production efficiency, enhancing specificity, quality and integrity.

## Future of Laboratories

The labs of the future will reflect the views of the scientific and academia communities about the approach that will be utilized to conduct clinical or research processes in the coming years. This will include a more digitized, automated and integrated workflow approach as compared to siloed methodologies currently being followed worldwide.

It will involve utilization of cutting-edge transformative technologies to drive the advancements in workflow, with impact on the current landscape as well as future evolution in terms of operation and performance. This could involve usage of virtual and sophisticated digital tools and advanced hardware, which can promote globalization of the lab environment in a more open, standardized and collaborative manner.

The labs of the future will be an integrated digital and physical facility with different software and hardware tools that simplify or automate data management and processes. Laboratory digitalization is complex and can have different scopes, depending on specific requirements. For example, a production line may be completely AI-driven, customer interaction can be online and paperless and/or a company may acquire another company with digital technology that fits into the long-term vision of the company.

## Startups and New Business Models

Advanced tech-based products and services by the startup community is transforming the healthcare landscape as we know it today. For example, British startup RescapeInnovation has developed immersive technologies to support patient care for all age groups. Leveraging VR distraction therapy facilitates better management of pain, anxiety and stress. For example, the solution offers cystic fibrosis patients the chance to view therapeutic documentaries where they can travel among the planets in the solar system or experience surfing, skydiving and other adrenaline-fueled activities, which has seen positive results in reducing anxiety in patients.[8]

Radmol AI is another startup in the industry that utilizes cloud computing, data analytics, blockchain and AI-based technology connecting patients and healthcare providers to local and global expert radiologists on demand. The platform facilitates access to reports anywhere and at any time, enabling patients, physicians and providers access to better healthcare systems.

## Healthcare in the Near Future

Over the next few years, integrated data sharing, heightened transparency for patients and predictive analytics will be paramount, as per Anthony Capone, president of DocGo, a leading AI-powered mobile healthcare service provider. Capone, in his article in *Forbes*,[9] brought forward the major challenges caused due to lack of data sharing. Some of them include lack of transparency, higher medical expenses and poor decision-making along with a series of other avoidable challenges. He states that secure sharing of patient data and information in compliance with the Health Insurance Portability and Accountability Act across medical providers will be one of the most important advancements in the coming decade, and healthcare technology companies have a massive opportunity to introduce the right tools to help both patients and providers in this context.

Technology adoption in the healthcare sector still has a long way to go and, therefore, health systems are focusing on

interim milestones to show value. In a Deloitte survey, 60 per
cent of the respondents indicated that their organizations are
midway through their journeys of digital transformation. The
healthcare system interviewees and panellists believe that the
transformation journey is longer than they had initially expected,
as the opportunities and definition of digital transformation
expand. Hence, there is a need to create frequent checkpoints
to measure the value of the initiatives, rather than wait until the
completion of the initiatives to measure returns on investments.

Today, the top players covered in the global digital healthcare
market include Medtronic, General Electric Company,
Cerner Corporation, McKesson Corporation, Infor, Allscripts,
Athenahealth, Inc., Diabetizer GmbH & Co. KG, Cognizant,
Dimensional Insight, Inc., Sie. According to *HIMSS Future of
Healthcare Report*, 80 per cent of healthcare providers plan to
increase investment in technology and digital solutions over the
next five years.

At the HIMSS22 Healthcare Cybersecurity Forum, Erik
Decker, CISO at Intermountain Healthcare, said, 'We have moved
beyond data. It is not just about privacy and confidentiality
anymore. Cybersecurity is patient safety. Downtime means delay
of care, and delay of care means patient safety.'[10]

## Cybersecurity in the Healthcare Segment

Since the onset of the COVID-19 pandemic, healthcare facilities
have been among the top targets for ransomware attacks and
this is expected to continue due to the large amount of person-
sensitive data.[11] Media reports show that over ten million records
have been stolen of every type. These included social security
numbers, patient medical records, financial data, HIV test results
and also private details of medical donors. On average, 155,000

records are breached during an attack on the sector and some incidents have also reported a breach of over three million records.[12] Cybersecurity remains one of the biggest concerns of the healthcare system amid rapid digitalization in the last few years. To combat this issue, it requires the collaborative effort of the public and private sector organizations. High-end software security tools, better training of human resources, increased investments by healthcare organizations and enforcement of stricter laws and norms by governments are a must.

## Summary

Clinical advances and digital technologies are at an extraordinary crossroad that is pushing the frontiers of preventive, predictive and precision medicine, using AI, bioengineering, digitization of clinical trials and improved understanding of human pathogen control.

Just like the ECG sensor on your health app uses electrical sensors on the back of the wearable wristband to measure the health of the heart, EEG sensors embedded in earbuds can measure brain health and quantify brain activity, including cognitive decline over time.

In the early says of the COVID-19 pandemic, bioengineering and AI were extensively harnessed to understand the behaviour of the SARS-Cov2 virus to harness the advances in gene- and genome-editing at scale to accelerate the development of diagnostic tests, medicines and vaccines. Genetic medicine is already being used to detect the risk of ALS with high predictivity. ALS, short for amyotrophic lateral sclerosis, is a progressive neurogenerative disease in which nerve cells break down and reduce muscle function. Though when the disease will occur can't be predicted, early risk-assessment will help in its treatment.

Scientists in Italy have published studies on AI-driven non-invasive and cost effective systems based on machine learning which is meant to support automated diagnosis of anaemia to high degree of accuracy. Traditional methods used to detect anaemia consist of blood tests and physical examination of the pallor of the fingertips, palms, nail beds and eye conjunctiva. The new system has been trained on a data set that derives from eye conjunctiva photos of Indian and Italian patients.

'The proposed system uses a low-cost device, which makes it suitable for widespread use. The performance of the learning algorithms utilizing two different areas of the mucous membrane of the eye is discussed. In particular, the RUSBoost algorithm, when appropriately trained on palpebral conjunctiva images, shows good performance in classifying anemic and nonanemic patients. The results are very robust, even when considering different ethnicities,' write researchers from Italy.[13]

As always, data protection is vital, more so when it is to do with human biology, as the potential for misuse is exponential, says legal ethicist Nita A. Farahany, distinguished professor of law and philosophy at Robinson O. Everett and founding director of the Initiative for Science and Society at Duke University. Dr Megan J. Palmer, the executive director of Bio Policy and Leadership Initiatives and adjunct professor in the Department of Bioengineering at Stanford University, underscored the need for responsible development in biotechnology to ensure the advances in synthetic biology and to not widen the gap in access to quality healthcare. Dr Palmer, who cochairs the World Economic Forum Global Future Council in Synthetic Biology, was at the WEF 2023 session on Transforming Medicine, Redefining Life in Davos along with Farahany.[14]

Surgeons at the operating table are already using a range of automated support systems. While human intervention will remain critical, it will devolve into a supervisory role while ensuring that patients' information is protected. Digital twin, gene editing and futuristic labs will help crack unsolvable challenges at an accelerated pace. Humans will get better healthcare even if most of it is provided by machines.

# 9

# Weapons of Mass Disruption

Every few months, a set of new technology phrases and jargon dominate conversations and debates. The pace of change indicates that civil society has to be far more aligned with new innovations that are set to influence the future of humankind in several possible ways.

With the march of technology accelerating, the Institute of Engineering and Technology has identified the top five new technologies that will impact businesses and even our personal lives over the next few months. These are broadly immersive technologies and metaverse, non-fungible token (NFT)/ tokenization and decentralized identity, DNA-based digital twin, decision intelligence, generative artificial intelligence (AI) and satellite communications. Developed using a combination of innovative ideas and significant improvements over the current

156

options, these technologies are set to dominate and impact nearly every sector in the coming years. Here is a quick look at what to expect from each of them.

## Immersive Technologies and Metaverse

Even as AR and VR are growing rapidly with increasing business applications, many versions and levels have created the overarching concept of extended reality or XR. According to computing firm HP, 'XR tech takes the human-to-PC screen interface and modifies it, either by (i) immersing in the virtual environment (VR), (ii) adding to, or augmenting, the user's surroundings (AR) or (iii) both of those (mixed reality).' In XR, X also stands for the new emerging technologies that allow higher levels of realistic immersive experience. These will have applications in what is called metaverse or digital universe.

From independent pockets of immersive experience and digital activities, the metaverse can connect all digital activities with each other. For instance, online gaming to medical data to travel planning can form a person's metaverse. It also allows people to engage with the digital universe of others for a shared experience. Metaverse is a combination of immersiveness, blockchain, NFTs, crypto, 5G/6G, voice and visual search, AI and interactive versions of the web.

## NFT/Tokenization and Decentralized Identity

The concept of decentralized identity will manifest itself in several ways. On business opportunity and take-off parameters, these sets of technologies rank the highest. However, the regulations on blockchain and cryptos are yet to mature. Microsoft describes decentralized identity as 'a trust framework in which identifiers, such as usernames, can be replaced with

IDs that are self-owned, independent and enable data exchange using blockchain and distributed ledger technology to protect the privacy and secure transactions.'

*Collins English Dictionary* selected NFT as the word of the year for 2021. As described by Collins, NFT is 'a unique digital certificate, registered in a blockchain, that is used to record the ownership of an asset such as an artwork or a collectible.' Such tokens are a symbol of a new form of identifying objects and people.

## DNA-Based Digital Twins

COVID-19-related research has pushed DNA-based innovation to new levels. Scientists can now produce a digital twin of a human to improve their understanding of a complex body system. Digital versions of humans are created from the data generated by various diagnostic efforts. Information from multiple devices is stitched together and analysed for each individual, which then helps predict and fight diseases among other uses. 'Digital twin computing initially starts with the extremely accurate reproduction of real-world human beings and things in cyberspace,' according to Japan's tech giant NTT's R&D division. It further adds, 'Digital twins are already being developed for a variety of applications in different industrial sectors, such as in the automobile sector, for autonomous driving; the robotic control sector and the medical sector.'

## Decision Intelligence and Generative Artificial Intelligence

AI will get smarter and sharper and humans will work far more collaboratively with it for rapid and complex decision-making. Similarly, generative AI will be a way more creative version

Weapons of Mass Disruption

of AI. It will be able to create content using existing information and images to match human output. Decision intelligence will be the improved version of AI, which includes social nuances, real-world complications and humanized approach. Such AI will go beyond pure numbers and data-based results to concept-based output. The various biases built into AI will be mitigated by non-data inputs.

## Satellite Communications

Rising investments and supportive policies will bring connectivity to every part of India. The corporate world will use satellite-based information at a higher scale with applications such as drones and global positioning system-based consumer solutions. Such connectivity will enable the usage of all other technologies.

In addition to these advancements, megatrends that are already redefining every industry such as quantum computing, edge computing, cloud computing and AR–VR technologies are going to witness wider and larger applications.

Let us consider quantum computing. Billions of dollars of investment are being made on a concept that still confounds most people. While quantum computing has been around for decades, since 2020, there has been enhanced interest from both investors and the government.

Quantum computing uses principles of physics in which sub-atomic qubits store and process information in a way that traditional computers cannot. The scale and speed of quantum computing are far ahead of what even a supercomputer can achieve. Some tasks that a classical computer may take a week to complete can be done in just one second with quantum computing.

Till late 2021, the governments of eighteen countries committed about US$25 billion in quantum computing initiatives according to a talent and training firm, Qureca.[1]

This also includes the Indian government as it has committed more than US$1 billion to National Mission on Quantum Technologies and Applications.

Private investment has grown too. More than US$1 billion was invested by venture funds in various quantum computing companies in 2021 alone.

In January 2023, Canada's prime minister Justin Trudeau announced a new federal investment of $40 million 'to enable the Toronto-based Canadian quantum computing company Xanadu Quantum Technologies Inc. to build and commercialize the world's first photonic-based, fault-tolerant quantum computer.'

Quantum research and consulting firm GQI, tracking government-funded projects by agencies and institutes for a number of countries, reported a total of more than $55 billion in state-sponsored research and development initiatives worldwide.[2]

'Quantum computing is an inherently multidisciplinary field, spanning a diverse range of disciplines from physics and mathematics to engineering and computer science. Quantum computing programs globally also involve a broad range of stakeholders across government, industry, academia and civil society,' says a new report by World Economic Forum (WEF) on quantum computing governance principles. The core principles that the WEF has identified include privacy, cybersecurity, open innovation and sustainability. A set of core values have also been identified to prevent human biases and ensure responsible behaviour. The report highlights that quantum computing must have 'mechanisms in place to ensure human accountability, both in its design and in its uses and outcomes'. Similar questions and challenges have arisen in the decision made by AI-based algorithms. Establishing human accountability for computing decisions is a matter of intense debate among regulators globally. Such principles and values become critical while considering the multi-industry applications of quantum computing. Companies like IBM have deployed it for several solutions. For example, it has worked with Mercedes-Benz to enhance the quality of batteries for electric vehicles. Scientists are keen to simulate the working of a battery at a molecular level to help improve efficiency. Simulating chemical reactions, interactions of millions of electrons and their impact can take a fraction of the time when done with quantum computing. Designing more efficient batteries can be accelerated by years as is being done by IBM. According to the company, it has more than twenty-seven quantum computers across the world 'running over 2 billion executions' a day.[3]

Quantum computing has tremendous use in the pharmaceutical sector as well. From drug discovery to vaccine trials, several efforts can be enhanced, improved and fast-tracked. Financial regulators hope to use this to keep track of increasingly complex and fast-paced digital transactions. Credit risk analysis, which includes several more parameters, can become far more accurate.

Even systems of national security, especially cyber threats, will be enhanced by quantum science. Its wide impact is becoming increasingly apparent to all stakeholders. However, the complex nature of quantum science needs deeper linkages between academia, scientists, governments, tech companies and investors.

India and other emerging economies must now invest in the talent required to fuel quantum science. Global power is now defined by technological abilities and not just military and economic strength. While India has committed to quantum computing, success will require multidimensional effort, which involves skilling as well as industry linkages. From supercomputers to quantum computing is still a big leap.

Quantum computer software, with several other technologies, needs immense computation power, such as machine learning (ML) and 5G, to help increase the computing speed, particularly in the banking, financial services and insurance (BFSI) and healthcare industries.

While rapid advancements in quantum technology have helped solve complex computational problems in a significantly lesser amount of time, building a new quantum computer is highly expensive. Thus quantum computing software can help organizations experiment with it. Startups are increasingly offering software solutions. D-wave is the earliest quantum start-up and the first company to sell a commercial quantum computer.

The technology is being deployed as a service so that researchers, physicists and consulting companies worldwide can develop a large number of applications and explore the possibilities for providing quantum solutions in the market. For instance, IBM has several real quantum devices and simulators available for use as a service. These devices are accessed and used through Qiskit, an open-source quantum software development kit, and IBM Q Experience, which offers a virtual interface for coding a quantum computer.

As can be seen in the estimated numbers from MarketsandMarkets, the quantum computing segment is growing steadily. The application segment of the quantum computing software market is projected to grow from US$114 million in 2021 to US$431 million by 2026, registering a CAGR of 30.5 per cent from 2021 to 2026. The optimization segment of the quantum computing software market was valued at US$52 million in 2021 and is expected to be US$181 million by 2026. The ML segment of the quantum computing software market is estimated to reach US$64 million by 2026 from US$15 million in 2021, registering a CAGR of 34.3 per cent during the forecast period.

From the sectoral side, the BFSI vertical is reckoned to dominate the quantum computing software market, reaching a market size of US$146.95 by 2026, at a CAGR of 30.9 per cent during the forecast period. In terms of region, North America is expected to be valued at US$45.8 million in 2021 and reach US$154.0 million by 2026, registering a CAGR of 27.5 per cent from 2021 to 2026, while Asia–Pacific (APAC) is expected to hold the largest market share by 2026. APAC is expected to be valued at US$37.9 million in 2021 and reach US$168.0 million by 2026, exhibiting a CAGR of 34.7 per cent from 2021 to 2026.

The significant growth of the quantum computing software market in APAC can be attributed to the increasing demand for quantum computing solutions and services in emerging economies such as China and South Korea for use in different applications. While quantum computing is a promising new technology, for application areas across industries, it may also pose a serious threat to the cybersecurity systems on which virtually all companies rely. Presently, most online-account passwords, as well as secure transactions and communications, are protected through encryption algorithms such as RSA (Rivest-Shamir-Adleman) or SSL/TLS (secure sockets layer/transport layer security). These systems make it easy for businesses to create data that can be shared by authorized users while also being protected from outsiders. As quantum computers can perform multiple calculations simultaneously, they have the potential to break any classical encryption system.

## Cloud Computing

The adoption of cloud-based solutions is well established now. An important dimension of this development is the rising popularity of private cloud services.

Simply put, when an individual or institution keeps information in a server located in a remote location, the service is called a cloud solution. Essentially, the servers where the data is stored are not within the premises of the company. Typically, companies rent space with cloud service providers who ensure constant access and relevant backup for their information with standard security measures.

The need for private cloud services has been rising in India and globally for a few critical reasons, especially because of the intensifying need for protecting data and taking ownership of its storage. Again, in simple terms, a private cloud means that a company has control over the server and the location where its data is stored.

In a normal cloud solution, the data can be kept wherever the service provider finds it convenient. A company may be sure of its data on the cloud but is never sure where exactly the servers hosting its data are located. However, in a private cloud, a company owns its servers within a data centre. The company knows exactly where the server is hosting its data. It is like owning a part of the warehouse and being in charge of it. The shift has been driven partly by regulatory needs and partly by security considerations.

In recent times, many governments and regulatory bodies across the world are seeking data localization. Many private and public sector companies in India are adopting digital processes and prefer private cloud solutions. Financial services providers have been told by central banks and other regulators to store data of their retail customers within the country. As it is often impractical for them to set up their data centres, so they are moving towards a private cloud. Consequently, their information is managed efficiently by the cloud services provider, while they have control over the servers that are located at a specified location. The cloud computing market will grow from US$548 billion in 2022 to US$1240 billion by 2027.

## Edge Computing

Edge computing is a new approach to network architecture that eliminates the limitations of traditional cloud computing. The rise in the deployment of IoT across industries and the pervasive use of mobile devices have compelled companies to enhance their IT infrastructure with edge computing. Edge computing helps in leveraging the rising data and machine-to-machine capabilities of IoT.

Edge computing has emerged as a crucial element in every industry as it enables enterprises to monitor and track assets and customer data in real time. Businesses are using edge computing to improve their asset management and achieve predictive maintenance. This helps them save operational costs and increase profit margins, eventually making business processes more organized and standardized. Companies already using IoT and cloud services are continuously integrating edge computing in their IT infrastructure. It eliminates security risks (Distributed Denial of Service [DDoS]) of cloud computing and improves interoperability and compatibility among IoT devices.

Hence, edge computing has numerous applications in emerging areas and technologies, such as smart cities, autonomous vehicles and connected car infrastructure, AR and VR and IIoT.

With ubiquitous digitalization, the proliferation of data has been phenomenal. Every day, we create roughly 2.5 quintillion bytes of data. This exponential increase in data traffic requires higher network bandwidth, the absence of which can lead to incomprehensible network congestion and failures. Advantages of edge computing, such as low latency, high bandwidth and low power, enable enterprises to easily overcome these issues by moving data processing and analysis closer to the source. Instead of moving all the data directly to the centralized storage, local edge computing centres identify only vital and mission-critical data and sends it to the central data centre or cloud. On the other hand, local edge centres also offload workload by compiling and sending daily reports about the remaining data for long-term storage. Subsequently, this helps in reducing the data that traverses the network and thereby reduces network bottlenecks.

According to MarketsandMarkets estimates, the global edge computing market size was estimated to be US$36.5 billion in 2021 and is projected to reach US$87.3 billion by 2026, at a CAGR of 19 per cent. The growth of this market can be attributed to technology evolution, growth in enterprise customers, large-scale investment, rise in the use of bring your own device (BYOD) in modern business practices and rising demand for latency connectivity.

Next comes the edge AI. It is the ability to execute AI algorithms on devices such as IoT and edge devices that are close to the source of data. Edge computing utilizes the computing capabilities available on phones, sensors and other edge devices to load, train and infer ML models. In the absence of edge AI, computers rely on network-related components such as graphics processing units (GPUs), memory and CPUs to operate and also, cloud computing has been doing most of the heavy lifting for models such as face detection and language generation. As a result, a user's device would merely transmit the data; an image or a piece of text over a network to the service and let the service do its calculations. The results are then sent back to the user. With edge AI, data does not need to be sent over the network for another machine to do the processing. Instead, it can remain on location, and the device itself can handle the computations.

'Edge IoT devices can process operating conditions in a factory and even predict if a piece of machinery could breakdown, thus enabling companies to ensure that predictive maintenance is done to avoid large-scale damage and loss, adding that in the future, security cameras equipped with edge AI may not only capture videos but also be able to identify people and footfalls. As edge technology analyses data locally rather than in a faraway cloud delayed by long-distance communications, it responds to users' needs in real time,' says Vish Nandlall, the VP of Technology Strategy and Ecosystems at Dell Technologies.

The past decade has seen a different kind of chip emerge, specifically designed to handle tasks for AI. Some of these new AI chips include AMD's Accelerated Processing Unit (APU), iPhone's AI Chip, Google's Tensor Processing Unit (TPU) and Intel's Nervana.

Edge AI enhances video analytics, inspection process, product testing, predictive maintenance, troubleshooting and anticipating issues within a complex physical system. However, it has some drawbacks too and includes less computing power than cloud computing and variation in types of machines, which could result in a higher probability of failure. Furthermore, it is hard to implement edge AI on the existing IoT network.

## Digital Twin

A digital twin is a virtual representation of any product, process or system. It is based on massive, cumulative, real-time and real-world data measurements across an array of dimensions. Digital twins use the data obtained from sensors and algorithms for making reasonable projections about future processes. It also utilizes past or historical data for analysing and giving predictive analysis decisions based on previous patterns and scenarios. These measurements can create an evolving profile of an object or process in the digital world, which will help provide important insights into system performance and make decisions such as a change in product design or manufacturing process.

Digital twin technology generates a virtual model of a physical asset or system, which can reduce operating costs and help extend the life of equipment and assets. Designers and engineers use digital twins of physical assets in a simulation process to meet product and production requirements for years. It creates a simulated replica throughout the life cycle of an asset to monitor health and diagnose anomalies in the asset's performance. These replicas are then used with plant asset management solutions to optimize operational downtime, trigger pre-emptive maintenance and mitigate costly failures. For industrial manufacturers, this technology offers a digital model of the machinery to better understand the performance and potential value of those physical machines. These virtual models allow operators to understand the machinery and give control access through a wireless network.

With the growing adoption of IoT, the concept of digital twinning is becoming prominent in the market. Product design and development, machine and equipment health monitoring, predictive maintenance and dynamic optimization are the four prominent application areas of digital twin. The key factors driving its demand include the need for fast-paced innovations and solutions in the healthcare and pharmaceutical industries, especially in the post-pandemic world; changing the face of maintenance in various industries; and adopting digital twin technology to cope with future pandemics or health crises.

Additionally, the market is also anticipated to witness growth from untapped opportunities including implementation of digital twin in the manufacturing industry to handle several issues due to the spread of COVID-19 and increasing adoption of the fourth industrial revolution/smart manufacturing and IIoT.

The National Aeronautics and Space Administration (NASA) has been using digital twin for its space station and spacecraft since 2002. NASA was the early adopter of this technology in the aerospace and defence industry. It uses a digital twin to monitor and control the space stations and spacecraft, and ensure crew safety. Digital twin is also used in the designing of the company's systems. Only when the company gets the system performance according to the requirements does it physically manufacture it. 'The importance of digital twins is increasing as we seek alternatives for certification of structures so large that they cannot be fully evaluated in existing test facilities and autonomous systems that are not deterministic. The idea of a digital twin is not a new one. What is new is the scale, ordinality, and non-deterministic nature of the models that are critical to achieving NASA's goals,' says a NASA report.[4]

Digital twin in smart manufacturing in APAC was valued at US$517.9 million in 2021 and is projected to reach US$14.01 billion by 2027; it is expected to grow at a CAGR of 76.2 per cent during the forecast period. The deployment of a digital twin will help companies gather data and use it for driving specific business outcomes. Reduction in downtime can be achieved with the implementation of a digital twin. The data fetched is analysed concerning various parameters, and both preventive and predictive measures are proactively taken up to avoid any harm to a product, process and system, which would, in turn, help reduce downtime and consequently increase the overall efficiency.

## AR and VR: Mixed Realities

AR is an interactive, reality-based display environment that utilizes the capabilities of computer-generated sounds, texts and effects to enhance the real-world experience of users. It combines real and computer-based scenes and images to deliver a unified and enhanced view of the world, and thus the perception of users, and the information provided helps perform tasks in the real world. AR works on components such as displays, sensors and embedded electronic components. Apart from adding to reality, projecting information on top of what users are already seeing, it has several uses, especially in application areas such as gaming and entertainment, enterprise, retail, healthcare and automotive.

VR technology provides the user with a virtual environment with the help of computer hardware and software. It provides a fully immersive environment to interact with objects similar to those in the real world. VR completely replaces a user's view, immersing them within a computer-generated virtual environment. It works on components such as gesture recognition systems, sensors and embedded electronic components. The processor helps to execute the input and gives the user an output in which the user can perceive that the object is a part of the environment. VR technology has several uses, especially in applications such as military, consumer, training, education and retail.

According to MarketsandMarkets estimates, the global AR market is expected to be worth US$86.5 billion by 2027, growing at a CAGR of 28 per cent during the forecast period. The VR market is expected to be valued at US$28 billion by 2027, growing at a CAGR of 18.8 per cent during the forecast period. The use of immersive VR with enhanced user experience is expected to drive the growth of the VR market. The market's growth is also due to the early adoption of head-mounted displays in gaming and entertainment. The use of gesture-tracking devices provides additional features in VR devices. The surging demand for AR devices and applications in healthcare, growing demand for AR in retail and e-commerce sectors and increasing investments in the AR market are the major drivers for the AR market. The major countries adopting digital twin are the US, Germany, the UK and China.

In the near future, business models such as traditional gaming will be replaced by new AR–VR-based gaming. The major challenge faced by AR manufacturers is to provide a wide field of view (FOV). The FOV is defined as the extent of the observable world at any given moment. While ideally, a human eye has a visual field of approximately 200° horizontally and 135° vertically, currently, AR and VR are capable of providing a FOV of up to 90°. For AR devices to create immersive experiences, they must capture as much of the FOV as possible.

## Summary

By definition, the new technologies will scythe through everything that has preceded them. For a while the older and the new technologies may coexist, but it is more likely that the latter will trigger the rapid collapse of the former. Quantum computing could create breakthroughs for personal and industrial machines in ways that we may yet be unable to anticipate. Digital twin could become so common that the neighbourhood doctor may become an expert. It is difficult to prepare for sudden change, but being alive to the possibility of rapid obsolescence will be critical for business leaders.

# Epilogue

Everything can become obsolete. As Heraclitus had said, nothing is permanent but change. In today's world, rapid obsolescence is the new constant. Obsolescence is spreading rapidly across sectors, processes and products at an insidious rate. From complex machines to simple tools, nothing is above being replaced. No product or service will be unaffected. Even government processes and business functions will change. Consider this: even the humble nuts and bolts are not spared. They have been holding up machines, structures and sundry objects for centuries. Without nuts and bolts, our world would fall apart. Now they are ready to become obsolete. In the smart new age, a new range of fasteners are keeping it together for a range of sectors from healthcare to automotive to construction.

Adhesive tapes of various kinds are now the nuts and bolts of products, devices and vehicles. Non-metallic fasteners such as tapes have proved to be especially useful for joining non-symmetric surfaces. Additionally, such adhesives and tapes are significantly lighter and help reduce the overall weight of various products.

Often unnoticed, the fasteners are evolving rapidly with deep scientific research and technological advancements. The manufacture and use of adhesive tapes is an invisible but smart disruption taking place in the industrial world. Investment in such products is rising across the world and is expected to accelerate in India too. Global material science giants along with domestic companies are increasing their investments in these new-age fasteners.

Futuristic videos show a world where gestures and voice command every action. Computing will be quantum and laptops will be malleable if not virtual.

Mobility could be by pods or underground loops. If they achieve the promise, the airline industry could see a severe shock. Creative destruction is the key to survival.

The fifth industrial revolution will involve deeper public–private collaborations. Global companies are committing to contribute to global public programmes that support social inclusion. 'Technology improves transparency. Many people say sunlight is the best antiseptic,' says Arvind Krishna, chairman and CEO of IBM. 'We often help our government clients in other countries. We can deploy banking systems, payment systems, social security, retirement, benefits, real-time payments—there's a lot of aspects where there is work to be done.'[1]

Take the passport for instance. The document of dreams, a passport, has undergone many transformations. From simple hand-written booklets to biometric-enabled, machine-readable documents, the passports across the world are poised for a dramatic shift.

Experts feel that a physical document may not even be required in the future. A combination of biometric information combined with national identity numbers could effectively be the new passport for crossing international borders.

This transition is happening in phases, though at a rapid pace. The first big shift is the move to chip-enabled e-passports. An e-passport is a document with an electronic chip embedded in a page. This chip keeps information such as the holder's name, date of birth, and other related information. The chip has a unique identification number and digital signature.

The next step for passports will go beyond the physical document to a digital identity-based system. Digital wallet IDs using blockchain and related technologies are being tried out in various projects. According to a research note by the French group Thales, much of the gate-keeping activity is done even before entering an airport terminal. A traveller will use a biometric on a digital ID wallet to create a Digital Travel Credential, which is then stored on a device.

Many countries have implemented versions of this near-future travel tech solution. International Air Travel Association (IATA) has been promoting the idea of One ID for a document-free travel process. 'One ID introduces an opportunity for the passenger to further streamline their journey with a document-free process based on identity management and biometric recognition. Passengers will be able to identify themselves at each airport touchpoint through a simple biometric recognition,' says IATA. This concept has been supported by the UN body International Civil Aviation Organization (ICAO) though the final solution will need larger collaboration with regulators across the world. ICAO has also begun assessment and coordination between various governments and agencies to bring a global standard for digital documents. Countries like the United Arab Emirates have introduced digital wallets as passports for certain categories of passengers. Other countries such as Australia and New Zealand are rolling out experimental projects with virtual identity documents. Once virtual documents take off, they will change the nature of identity. An entire industry based on identity documents will be replaced by a digital process.

It will be the survival of those who change faster than others. Those who are prepared for the changes will thrive. Those who can see around the corner and prepare for a new world will thrive. The rest will rest in peace. This is the US$25 trillion transition we are living in. What is more, we have demonstrated in this book that these changes are destroying old models even while creating new concepts in tech-led solutions.

It will not be out of place to say that the strongest force disrupting business models will not be technological breakthroughs alone. The biggest disruptor would be the need for making societies safer, productive and less harmful to the environment. Technology will be expected to disrupt business models to serve the society. Technological innovations will remain difficult to predict but their impact is easier to anticipate. Revenue and cost models will be rapidly and steadily evolve with technological changes and social demands.

Tackling harm created by digital activity is now a priority for governments worldwide. 'We are trying to reduce harm from happening by working with the technology industry and encouraging them to incorporate safety into the design and development of their products and services. The tech industry needs to take a more proactive and innovative approach and invest in safety as a core business interest,' says Julie Inman Grant, the esafety commissioner of Australia.[2]

Technology-led business model shifts will be deeply influenced by the principles of stakeholder capitalism. Founder and executive chairman of World Economic Forum, Professor Klaus Schwab says, 'Capitalism is a form of capitalism in which companies do not only optimize short-term profits for shareholders, but seek long term value creation, by taking into account the needs of all their stakeholders, and society at large.'[3]

# Notes and References

## Prologue

1   Details available at MSCI, 'ESG 101: What Is Environmental, Social and Governance?', https://www.msci.com/esg-101-what-is-esg
2   Details available at United Nations, 'The 17 Goals', https://sdgs.un.org/goals
3   Samir Saran and Sharad Sharma, 'Digital Public Infrastructure—Lessons from India', Observer Research Foundation, 7 February 2023, https://www.orfonline.org/research/digital-public-infrastructure-lessons-from-india/
4   Stephanie M. Noble, Martin Mende, Dhruv Grewal and A. Parasuraman, 'The Fifth Industrial Revolution: How Harmonious Human–Machine Collaboration is Triggering a Retail and Service [R]evolution', Journal of Retailing, Volume 98, Issue 2, June 2022, Pages 199–208, https://www.sciencedirect.com/science/article/pii/S0022435922000288#:~:text=The%20Fifth%20Industrial%20Revolution%2C%20or,companies%2C%20employees%2C%20customers

5    Pranjal Sharma, 'Productivity Needs Automation-First Mindset', *Business World*, 23 January 2023, https://www.businessworld.in/article/-Productivity-Needs-Automation-First-Mindset-/23-01-2023-462983/

6    'Building Safer Dialogue Agents', 22 September 2022, https://www.deepmind.com/blog/building-safer-dialogue-agents; Anthony Cuthbertson, 'DeepMind's AI Chatbot Can Do Things That ChatGPT Cannot, CEO Claims', 16 January 2023, https://www.independent.co.uk/tech/deepmind-ai-chatbot-chatgpt-openai-b2262862.html; Yusuf Mehdi, 'Reinventing Search with a New AI-Powered Microsoft Bing and Edge, Your Copilot for the Web', 7 February 2023, https://blogs.microsoft.com/blog/2023/02/07/reinventing-search-with-a-new-ai-powered-microsoft-bing-and-edge-your-copilot-for-the-web/

7    Federico Berruti et al., 'Intelligent Process Automation: The Engine at the Core of the Next-Generation Operating Model', 14 March 2017, https://www.mckinsey.com/capabilities/mckinsey-digital/our-insights/intelligent-process-automation-the-engine-at-the-core-of-the-next-generation-operating-model

8    Alan Schwarz, 'America's Best Management Consulting Firms', 15 March 2023, https://www.forbes.com/lists/best-management-consulting-firms/?sh=6172a3c32b87

## References

Cognizant website, glossary: https://www.cognizant.com/us/en/glossary/intelligent-process-automation#:~:text=Intelligent%20process%20automation%20(IPA)%E2%80%94,business%20process%20automation%20that%20thinks%2C

McKinsey Digital website: https://www.mckinsey.com/capabilities/mckinsey-digital/our-insights/intelligent-process-automation-the-engine-at-the-core-of-the-next-generation-operating-model

UiPath website: https://www.uipath.com/rpa/intelligent-process-automation

## Introduction

1    Nidhi Singal, 'How Digital Twins of Machines and Assets are Helping Industries Innovate', btMag, 12 June 2022, https://www.businesstoday.in/magazine/technology/story/how-digital-twins-of-machines-and-assets-are-helping-industries-innovate-336753-2022-06-08

## 1: Flying New Frontiers

1    George Whitesides, 'Where Will Space Technology Take Us by 2030, and What Does This Mean for Life on Earth?', World Economic Forum, 22 February 2017, https://www.weforum.org/agenda/2017/02/space/

2    Details available at Bonnie Dunbar, 'The Spacesuit Digital Thread: 4.0 Manufacture of Custom High Performance Spacesuits for the Exploration of Mars', NASA, 1 February 2022, https://www.nasa.gov/directorates/spacetech/niac/2022/Spacesuit_Digital_Thread/

3    Details available at James Wynbrandt, 'Space 2.0: The New Age of Extraterrestrial Exploration', Nasdaq, 2 June 2020, https://www.nasdaq.com/articles/space-2.0%3A-the-new-age-of-extraterrestrial-exploration-2020-06-02

4    Details available at Erick Burgueño Salas, 'Global Government Investment on Space Exploration by Type 2010–2029', Statista, 28 September 2022, https://www.statista.com/statistics/946361/space-exploration-government-expenditure-type-worldwide/

5    Douglas Insights, 'Satellite IoT Market is Estimated to Grow at CAGR of ~20%, 2021-2028 | Latest Industry Coverage by Douglas Insights', Global Newswire, 12 October 2022, https://www.globenewswire.com/en/news-release/2022/10/12/2532511/0/en/Satellite-IoT-Market-is-Estimated-to-Grow-at-CAGR-of-20-2021-2028-Latest-Industry-Coverage-by-Douglas-Insights.html

6    Samuel Gibbs and agencies, 'Elon Musk Wants to Cover the World with Internet from Space', *The Guardian*, 17 November 2016, https://www.theguardian.com/technology/2016/nov/17/elon-musk-satellites-internet-spacex

7    Darrell Etherington, 'Swarm Gets All the Approvals It Needs to Begin Operating Its Satellite Connectivity Service in the US', 6 April 2020, https://techcrunch.com/2020/04/06/swarm-gets-all-the-approvals-it-needs-to-begin-operating-its-satellite-connectivity-service-in-the-u-s/

8    Details available at Eric Brothers, '2022 Forecast', January–February 2022, https://www.aerospacemanufacturinganddesign.com/article/2022-forecast/

9    Details available at Diana Dimitrova, et al., 'The Growing Climate Stakes for the Defense Industry', BCG, 10 September 2021, https://www.bcg.com/publications/2021/growing-climate-stakes-for-the-defense-industry

10    Details available at John Coykendall, Steve Shepley and Aijaz Hussain, 'Decarbonizing Aerospace', Deloitte Insights, 7 October 2021, https://www2.deloitte.com/us/en/insights/industry/aerospace-defense/decarbonizing-aerospace.html/#industry

11    Details available at Accenture, 'Aerospace and Defense Technology Vision 2022', 23 May 2022, https://www.accenture.com/us-en/insights/aerospace-defense/tech-vision

12    Details available at Uri Pelli and Robin Riedel, 'Flying-Cab Drivers Wanted', McKinsey and Company, 2 June 2020, https://www.mckinsey.com/industries/automotive-and-assembly/our-insights/flying-cab-drivers-wanted

13    Details available at Benedikt Kloss and Robin Riedel, 'Up in the Air: How Do Consumers View Advanced Air Mobility?', McKinsey and Company, 1 June 2021, https://www.mckinsey.com/industries/aerospace-and-defense/our-insights/up-in-the-air-how-do-consumers-view-advanced-air-mobility

14    'Drone Taxi Take First Spin in Air Traffic Near Paris', Reuters 12 November 2022, https://www.reuters.com/lifestyle/science/drone-taxi-take-first-spin-air-traffic-near-paris-2022-11-10/

15    Details available at Caspar Henderson, 'A Record-Breaking Commercial-Scale Hydrogen Plane Has Taken Off in the UK, with More Set to Join It Soon. How Far Can Such Planes Go in Cutting the Aviation Industry's Emissions?', 8 April 2021, https://www.bbc.com/future/article/20210401-the-worlds-first-commercial-hydrogen-plane

16    https://hydrogen-central.com/zeroavia-birmingham-airport-plan-zero-emission-flights-hydrogen-powered-aviation/

17    https://www.zeroavia.com/first-flight-and-more

18    Details available at John Coykendall, Aijaz Hussain and Siddhant Mehra, 'Operationalizing Advanced Air Mobility', https://www2.deloitte.com/content/dam/Deloitte/us/Documents/energy-resources/Charticle-for-Advanced-Air_Mobility-031921.pdf

19    Details available at https://afwerx.com/agility-prime/#/

20    Christopher Prawdzik, 'Air Force Aims to Get More eVTOL Platforms into Testing, Exercises in 2023', Air and Space Forces Magazine, 9 January 2023, https://www.airandspaceforces.com/air-force-aims-to-get-more-evtol-platforms-into-testing-exercises-in-2023/

21    Details available at Flight Crowd, 'Urban Air Mobility Glossary', https://www.flight-crowd.com/estol

22    Details available at Avionics, 'Airbus Demos New Automated Aerial Refueling Technology', 12 May 2017, https://www.aviationtoday.

com/2017/05/12/airbus-demonstrates-new-automated-aerial-refueling-technology/

23  Details available at Harry Lye, 'Tomorrow's Tankers: The Future of Aerial Refuelling', Airforce Technology, 26 March 2020, https://www.airforce-technology.com/features/tomorrows-tankers-the-future-of-aerial-refuelling/

24  Details available at David Vergun, 'Aerial Refueling Adds Lethality to DOD Aviation', US Department of Defence, 21 February 2020, https://www.defense.gov/News/Feature-Stories/Story/Article/2089889/aerial-refueling-adds-lethality-to-dod-aviation/

25  Details available at Global Data, 'Electronic Warfare Market – Thematic Research', 04 October 2021, https://store.globaldata.com/report/electronic-warfare-market-analysis/

26  Andrea Cornell et al., 'Drones Take to the Sky, Potentially Disrupting Last-Mile Delivery', McKinsey and Company, 3 January 2023, https://www.mckinsey.com/industries/aerospace-and-defense/our-insights/future-air-mobility-blog/drones-take-to-the-sky-potentially-disrupting-last-mile-delivery

27  'Walmart Now Operates Drone Delivery in 7 States, Completes 6,000 Drone Deliveries', Business Wire, 05 January 2023, https://www.businesswire.com/news/home/20230105005929/en/Walmart-Now-Operates-Drone-Delivery-in-7-States-Completes-6000-Drone-Deliveries

28  CDOTrends editors, 'Amazon Completes First Drone Deliveries', CDOTrends, 17 January 2023, https://www.cdotrends.com/story/17780/amazon-completes-first-drone-deliveries

29  Katie Tarasov, 'A First Look at Amazon's New Delivery Drone, Slated to Start Deliveries This Year', 12 November 2022, https://www.cnbc.com/2022/11/11/a-first-look-at-amazons-new-delivery-drone.html

## 2: Planting in Air, Earth and Water

1  Details available at World Economic Forum, 'Using Technology to Improve a Billion Livelihoods', October 2022, https://www3.weforum.org/docs/WEF_Using_Technology_to_Improve_a_Billion_Livelihoods_2022.pdf

2  The Hindu, 'Krishi Vigyan Kendra Demonstrates Use of Drone Technology in Pesticide Application in Vriddhachalam', 20 April 2022, https://www.thehindu.com/news/national/tamil-nadu/krishi-vigyan-kendra-demonstrates-use-of-drone-technology-in-pesticide-application-in-vriddhachalam/article65337825.ece

184      Notes and References

184      Notes and References

184      Notes and References

184      Notes and References

14    Details available at SSI Schaefer, 'Improving Logistics Infrastructure to Meet the Growth in Asia's Food Sector', 18 October 2021, https://www.ssi-schaefer.com/en-th/best-practices-trends/trends/improving-logistics-infrastructure-to-meet-the-growth-in-asia-s-food-sector-884944

15    Details available at Asia Pacific Food Industry, 'Sustainable F&B Logistics—The Warehousing Approach', 20 September 2017, https://www.apfoodonline.com/industry/sustainable-fb-logistics-the-warehousing-approach/?__cf_chl_f_tk=vLxJqJsa.tDtd48LC7qEiT28Bpn5gL85hXFDI3CB1TA-1642428875-0-gaNycGzNCL0

16    Details available at Fact.MR, 'Automated Storage and Retrieval Systems Market', https://www.factmr.com/report/1869/automated-storage-and-retrieval-systems-market

17    Details available at Elizabeth Elkin, Mai Ngoc Chau & Agnieszka de Sousa, 'Your Food Prices Are at Risk as the World Runs Short of Workers', 2 September 2021, https://www.bloombergquint.com/global-economics/food-prices-driven-up-by-global-worker-shortage-brexit

18    Details available at Marcus Casey and Ember Smith, 'Automation from Farm to Table: Technology's Impact on the Food Industry', Brookings, 23 November 2020, https://www.brookings.edu/blog/up-front/2020/11/23/automation-from-farm-to-table-technologys-impact-on-the-food-industry/

19    Details available at McKinsey Digital, 'Where Machines Could Replace Humans—and Where They Can't (Yet)', 8 July 2016, https://www.mckinsey.com/business-functions/mckinsey-digital/our-insights/where-machines-could-replace-humans-and-where-they-cant-yet

20    Details available at *The Economic Times*, 'Laying the Groundwork for a Food Secure Future', 20 December 2021, https://economictimes.indiatimes.com/news/international/uae/laying-the-groundwork-for-a-food-secure-future/articleshow/88392050.cms

21    Details available at Swetha Kolluri, Krishnan S. Raghavan and Rozita Singh, 'Accelerating Agri-tech to Transform Food Systems', 10 January 2022, https://www.dailypioneer.com/2022/columnists/accelerating-agri-tech-to-transform-food-systems.html

## References

India Brand Equity Foundation, 'Future of Indian Food and Beverage Industry Post-Pandemic', 3 December 2020, https://www.ibef.org/blogs/future-of-indian-food-and-beverage-industry-post-pandemic

Jon Markman, 'Disruptive Farmers Grow a New Age Business Model', *Forbes*, 19 January 2019, https://www.forbes.com/sites/jonmarkman/2019/01/19/disruptive-farmers-grow-a-new-ag-business-model/?sh=30ef46a83a21

## 3: The Chemistry of Chemicals

1   David L. Chandler, 'Engineers Develop a New Kind of Shape-Memory Material', MIT News, 5 October 2022, https://news.mit.edu/2022/shape-memory-material-ceramic-1005

2   Details available at McKinsey and Company, 'The State of the Chemical Industry—It Is Getting More Complex', 10 November 2020, https://www.mckinsey.com/industries/chemicals/our-insights/the-state-of-the-chemical-industry-it-is-getting-more-complex

3   Details available at Deloitte, '2023 Chemical Industry Outlook', https://www2.deloitte.com/us/en/pages/energy-and-resources/articles/chemical-industry-outlook.html

4   Details available at https://www.treehugger.com/green-chemistry-environment-4859473

5   Details available at American Chemical Society, 'Sustainable Denim Manufacturing Process Creates "Green" Jeans', 19 June 2012, https://phys.org/news/2012-06-sustainable-denim-green-jeans.html

6   Details available at P&S Intelligence, 'Green Chemicals Market to Grow With 6.6% CAGR by 2030: P&S Intelligence', 24 March 2021, https://www.prnewswire.com/news-releases/green-chemicals-market-to-grow-with-6-6-cagr-by-2030-ps-intelligence-301254649.html

7   Details available at World Economic Forum, 'Digital Transformation of Industries', 22 January 2016, https://reports.weforum.org/digital-transformation/wp-content/blogs.dir/94/mp/files/pages/files/dti-chemistry-and-advanced-materials-industry-white-paper.pdf

8   Details available at World Economic Forum, 'Three Ways Digital Innovation Is Revolutionizing Chemistry and Advanced Materials', 21 September 2016, https://www.weforum.org/agenda/2016/09/three-ways-digital-innovation-is-revolutionizing-chemistry-advanced-materials/

9   Details available at PWC, Chemicals Trends 2020: Winning Strategies for an Era of Sustainable Value Chains', https://www.pwc.com/gx/en/ceo-survey/2020/trends/chemicals-trends-2020.pdf

10  Details available at World Economic Forum, 'Digital Transformation of Industries', 22 January 2016, https://reports.weforum.org/digital-

transformation/wp-content/blogs.dir/94/mp/files/pages/files/dti-
chemistry-and-advanced-materials-industry-white-paper.pdf

11   Accenture, 'The Remaking of Industries', https://www.accenture.
com/_acnmedia/thought-leadership-assets/pdf-2/accenture-
remaking-industries-chemicals-pdf-report.pdf

12   Details available at Bioforce, 'From Waste to Well-Being: CH-Bioforce
Helps World's Biggest Brewing Company Turn Brewing Waste into
Textiles', press release, 2 April 2020, https://www.ch-bioforce.com/
wp-content/uploads/CH-Bioforce-press-release-en-02042020.pdf

13   Details available at Coatings World, 'Green Coatings', https://www.
coatingsworld.com/issues/2017-11-01/view_features/green-coatings/

14   Details available at Adhesive Platform, 'Sustainable Adhesives', https://
www.adhesiveplatform.com/sustainability-of-adhesives-and-sealants/

15   Details available at Accenture, 'Chemical Customers Are Ready to Buy
More, Pay More', 30 October 2020, https://www.accenture.com/us-
en/insights/chemicals/chemical-customers-ready-buy-more-pay-more

16   Details available at McKinsey and Company, 'How Chemical Players
Can Win in the Transition to Digital Platforms', 1 March 2021,
https://www.mckinsey.com/industries/chemicals/our-insights/how-
chemical-players-can-win-in-the-transition-to-digital-platforms

17   Details available at CDI Energy Products, 'Aerospace Industry', https://
www.cdiproducts.com/solutions/markets/aerospace

18   Details available at GE Additive, 'Aviation and Aerospace Industry',
https://www.ge.com/additive/additive-manufacturing/industries/
aviation-aerospace

## 4: Smart Manufacturing Advances Further

1   Rockwell Automation, *Enabling Sustainability*, 2022, https://www.
rockwellautomation.com/en-us/company/about-us/sustainability/
report.html#gate-c106c9cc-4db7-4bce-9157-cad89e51aab0

2   Details available at McKinsey and Company, 'COVID-19: An
Inflection Point for Industry 4.0', 15 January 2021, https://www.
mckinsey.com/business-functions/operations/our-insights/covid-19-
an-inflection-point-for-industry-40

3   Details available at Jitendra Soni, 'Over the Air Charging across the
Room Could Be a Reality This Year', 28 April 2022, https://www.
techradar.com/in/news/over-the-air-charging-across-the-room-
could-be-a-reality-this-year

4   Details available at Cesar Johnston, '5 Breakthroughs Paving the Way
for the Future of Wireless Charging', *EE Times*, https://www.eetasia.

com/5-breakthroughs-paving-the-way-for-the-future-of-wireless-charging/

5   Details available at Manufacturing, 'Drone Development in the Manufacturing Sector', 17 May 2020, https://manufacturingdigital. com/technology/drone-development-manufacturing-sector

6   Details available at Metrology.News, 'Drones in the Factory of the Future', https://metrology.news/drones-in-the-factory-of-the-future/

7   Details available at MarketsandMarkets, 'Collaborative Robot Market', https://www.marketsandmarkets.com/Market-Reports/collaborative-robot-market-194541294.html

8   Details available at Dan Monk, 'Local Companies Cozy Up to Robots in Tight Labor Market', https://www.wcpo.com/money/local-business-news/local-companies-cozy-up-to-robots-in-tight-labor-market

9   Zach Thompson, 'Vinpac Chooses Dematic AGVs for Efficient Operations', 25 January 2023, https://itbrief.com.au/story/vinpac-chooses-dematic-agvs-for-efficient-operations

10  Details available at Jason Walker, 'AMR vs AGV: A Clear Choice for Flexible Material Handling', Locus Robotics, https://waypointrobotics.com/blog/amr-vs-agv/

11  Details available at Semiconductor Industry Association, '2022 State of the US Semiconductor Industry', https://www.semiconductors.org/state-of-the-u-s-semiconductor-industry/

12  Details available at Deloitte, '2023 Semiconductor Industry Outlook', https://www2.deloitte.com/us/en/pages/technology-media-and-telecommunications/articles/semiconductor-industry-outlook.html

## Other Resources

Deloitte, '2023 Semiconductor Industry Outlook', https://www2.deloitte. com/us/en/pages/technology-media-and-telecommunications/articles/semiconductor-industry-outlook.html

Ewelina Gregolinska et al., 'Capturing the True Value of Industry 4.0', McKinsey and Company, https://www.mckinsey.com/capabilities/operations/our-insights/capturing-the-true-value-of-industry-four-point-zero

MarketsandMarkets, 'Artificial Intelligence (Chipsets) Market', https://www.marketsandmarkets.com/Market-Reports/artificial-intelligence-chipset-market-237558655.html

Matteo Mancini, et al., 'Industry 4.0 Adoption with the Right Focus', McKinsey and Company, https://www.mckinsey.com/business-functions/operations/our-insights/operations-blog/industry-40-adoption-with-the-right-focus

McKinsey and Company, 'Toward Smart Production: Machine Intelligence in Business Operations', 1 February 2022, https://www.mckinsey.com/business-functions/operations/our-insights/toward-smart-production-machine-intelligence-in-business-operations

Meghan Rimol, 'What Intel's $20B Chip Factory Investment Says About the Future of the Semiconductor Market', Gartner, https://www.gartner.com/en/articles/what-intel-s-20b-chip-factory-investment-says-about-the-future-of-the-semiconductor-market

World Economic Forum, 'Manufacturing Reimagined: From Improved Productivity to Profitable Growth', 18 January 2021, https://www.weforum.org/agenda/2021/01/manufacturing-reimagined-from-improved-productivity-to-profitable-growth/

## 5: Automotive for the People

1   Rebecca Bellan, 'Motional Opens Las Vegas Robotaxi Service to Nighttime Hours', Joint Tech Crunch, 23 February 2023, https://techcrunch.com/2023/02/23/motional-las-vegas-robotaxi-uber-lyft-night-rides/

2   'Motional Launches First Robotaxi Service on the Uber Network', 7 December 2022, https://motional.com/news/motional-launches-first-robotaxi-service-uber-network

3   Details available at Doug Ertz, 'One in Five Automotive Industry Leaders See Intelligent Systems as the Future Predominant Business Model', *Forbes*, https://www.forbes.com/sites/windriver/2021/10/01/one-in-five-automotive-industry-leaders-see-intelligent-systems-as-the-future-predominant-business-model/?sh=e51777e4fa0a

4   Details available at Technavio, 'Connected Car Market to Grow at a CAGR of 26.26% by 2025: Increasing Internet Penetration and Its Impact on the Connected Cars Market to Boost Growth—17000+ Technavio Reports', 23 November 2021, https://www.prnewswire.com/news-releases/connected-car-market-to-grow-at-a-cagr-of-26-26-by-2025--increasing-internet-penetration--its-impact-on-the-connected-cars-market-to-boost-growth--17000-technavio-reports-301430401.html

5    Steve Tengler, 'Top 25 Auto Cybersecurity Hacks: Too Many Glass Houses To Be Throwing Stones', 30 June 2020, https://www.forbes.com/sites/stevetengler/2020/06/30/top-25-auto-cybersecurity-hacks-too-many-glass-houses-to-be-throwing-stones/?sh=22196e1a7f65

6    Details available at MarketsandMarkets, 'Augmented Reality Automotive Market', https://www.marketsandmarkets.com/Market-Reports/automotive-augmented-reality-market-126800260.html#:~:text=The%20augmented%20reality%20automotive%20market%20is%20projected%20to%20grow%20at,USD%206.79%20Billion%20by%202025.

7    Details available at Goldman Sachs, 'Cars 2025', https://www.goldmansachs.com/insights/technology-driving-innovation/cars-2025/

8    Details available at Aria Alamalhodaei, 'General Motors' New Software Platform Ultifi Is Coming to Vehicles Starting in 2023', Joint Techcrunch, 30 September 2021, https://techcrunch.com/2021/09/29/general-motors-new-software-platform-ultifi-is-coming-to-vehicles-starting-in-2023/

9    Details available at Dick Slansky, 'Manufacturing Trends and Technologies in the Automotive Industry', Automation World, 5 August 2021, https://www.automationworld.com/business-intelligence/article/21579012/manufacturing-trends-and-technologies-in-the-automotive-industry

10   Details available at McKinsey and Company, 'The Case for an End-to-End Automotive-Software Platform', 16 January 2020, https://www.mckinsey.com/industries/automotive-and-assembly/our-insights/the-case-for-an-end-to-end-automotive-software-platform

11   Details available at CNBC TV18, 'Here Are 7 Most Exciting Tech Innovations That Will Drive the EV Revolution', 9 February 2022, https://www.cnbctv18.com/auto/here-are-7-most-exciting-tech-innovations-that-will-drive-the-ev-revolution-12425312.htm

12   Biliti Electric, 'Battery Swapping: The Game-Changing Technology For Electric Vehicles', https://bilitielectric.com/blog/ev-battery-swap/

13   Details available at World Economic Forum, 'Why the Future for Cars Is Connected', 8 July 2021, https://www.weforum.org/agenda/2021/07/why-the-future-for-cars-is-connected/

14   Details available at Szabolcs Fulop, 'Occupancy Status Technology: Is It the Future of Vehicle Safety?, 6 April 2022, https://www.electronicdesign.com/markets/automotive/article/21238220/xperi-occupancy-status-technology-is-it-the-future-of-vehicle-safety

15    Details available at Capgemini, 'How Automotive Organizations Can Maximize the Smart Factory Potential', https://www.capgemini. com/resources/automotive-smart-factories/#:~:text=Automotive%20 Smart%20Factories%3A%20Putting%20Auto,Digital%20Industrial%20 Revolution%20Driving%20Seat&text=Drawing%20on%20a%20 survey%20of,productivity%20gains%20by%202023%20onwards.

16    Details available at https://www.packworld.com/home/ article/21579012/manufacturing-trends-and-technologies-in-the-automotive-industry

17    Details available at McKinsey and Company, 'Amid Disruption, Automotive Suppliers Must Reimagine Their Footprints', 19 April 2022, https://www.mckinsey.com/industries/automotive-and-assembly/our-insights/amid-disruption-automotive-suppliers-must-reimagine-their-footprints

18    Details available at Forbes, 'The New Auto Industry: Change And Innovation For A Sustainable World', 12 January 2021, https://www. forbes.com/sites/sap/2021/01/12/the-new-auto-industry-change-and-innovation-for-a-sustainable-world/?sh=74da276d56c7

19    Details available at Automotive World, 'Four Trends Transforming the Automotive Industry', 28 January 2022, https://www.automotiveworld. com/articles/four-trends-transforming-the-automotive-industry/

20    Details available at Marcela De Vivo, 'Experts Predict Massive Growth in Augmented Reality in Automotive Industry', Relay Cars, 5 October 2020, https://blog.relaycars.com/massive-growth-augmented-reality-automotive/

21    Cedric Jackson, 'Top Trends to Expect from Carmakers in 2023', Auto Service World, 1 February 2023, https://www.autoserviceworld.com/ top-trends-to-expect-from-carmakers-in-2023/

22    Ford Media Centre, 'Ford, Argo AI, and Walmart to Launch Autonomous Vehicle Delivery Service in Three U.S. Cities', https:// media.ford.com/content/fordmedia/fna/us/en/news/2021/09/15/ ford-argo-ai-and-walmart.html

23    Ryan Jones, 'Potential Solutions to the First Mile/Last Mile Problem', https://futurist.law.umich.edu/potential-solutions-to-the-first-mile-last-mile-problem/

## 6: Vectors of Changing Sectors

1    Saurav Anand, 'NHAI Lays Down Procedures for Extensive Road Safety Audits', Mint, 14 January 2023, https://www.livemint.com/

news/india/nhai-lays-down-procedures-for-extensive-road-safety-audits-11673696741245.html

2    https://auto.economictimes.indiatimes.com/news/industry/total-toll-collection-through-fastag-grows-46-pc-to-rs-50855-crore-in-2022-nhai/97345936

3    Details available at GSA, '5G-Market Snapshot June 2022', https://gsacom.com/paper/5g-market-snapshot-june-2022/

4    Details available at Simon Read, '5G Signals Dawn Of New Era For Mobile Communications', Forbes Advisor, 24 March 2022, https://www.forbes.com/uk/advisor/mobile-phones/5g-signals-dawn-of-new-era-for-mobile-communications/

5    Details available at Cisco, 'What Is Wi-Fi 6?', https://www.cisco.com/c/en_in/products/wireless/what-is-wi-fi-6.html

6    Details available at The National Security Commission on Artificial Intelligence, 'The Final Report', https://www.nscai.gov/2021-final-report/

7    Details available at Centre for Strategic and International Studies, 'The Collection Edge: Harnessing Emerging Technologies for Intelligence Collection', https://www.csis.org/analysis/collection-edge-harnessing-emerging-technologies-intelligence-collection

## 7: Firing Up Green Digital Energy

1    Details available at Anmar Frangoul, 'UK Trial Will Inject Hydrogen into a Gas-Fired, Grid-Connected Power Station', *CNBC*, 26 October 2022, https://www.cnbc.com/2022/10/26/uk-trial-will-inject-hydrogen-into-a-gas-fired-grid-connected-power-station.html; https://www.centrica.com/media-centre/news/2022/centrica-and-hiiroc-to-inject-hydrogen-at-brigg-gas-fired-power-station-in-uk-first-project/

2    Details available at MarketsandMarkets, 'Making Cities EV Ready', https://www.marketsandmarkets.com/disruptiondialogues/Making-Cities-EV.asp

3    Details available at World Economic Forum, 'Harnessing Artificial Intelligence to Accelerate the Energy Transition', white paper, September 2021, https://www3.weforum.org/docs/WEF_Harnessing_AI_to_accelerate_the_Energy_Transition_2021.pdf

4    Details available at IoT for All, '4 Ways IoT and Data Science Are Being Used to Fight Climate Change', 2 August 2019, https://www.iotforall.com/4-ways-iot-data-science-fight-climate-change

5     Details available at McKinsey and Company, 'Digital Transformation in Energy: Achieving Escape Velocity', 3 September 2020, https://www.mckinsey.com/industries/oil-and-gas/our-insights/digital-transformation-in-energy-achieving-escape-velocity

6     Details available at IEA, 'Digitalisation and Energy', November 2017, https://www.iea.org/reports/digitalisation-and-energy

7     Details available at Warwick Goodall et al., 'The Rise of Mobility as a Service', Deloitte Review, Issue 20, https://www2.deloitte.com/content/dam/Deloitte/nl/Documents/consumer-business/deloitte-nl-cb-ths-rise-of-mobility-as-a-service.pdf

8     Details available at Clint Bradford, 'The Future of Intelligent Building Energy Management Systems Relies on Smart Strategies', https://www.buildingsiot.com/blog/the-future-of-intelligent-building-energy-management-systems-relies-on-smart-strategies-bd

9     Details available at World Economic Forum, 'How to Build Smart, Zero Carbon Buildings—and Why It Matters', 8 September 2021, https://www.weforum.org/agenda/2021/09/how-to-build-zero-carbon-buildings/

10    Details available at Joe Kuehne, '4 Tech Trends to Watch in Energy and Utilities in 2022', Biz Tech, 10 December 2021, https://biztechmagazine.com/article/2021/12/4-tech-trends-watch-energy-and-utilities-2022

11    Details available at Plug and Play, '9 Emerging Technologies in Utilities of the Future to Keep an Eye On', https://www.plugandplaytechcenter.com/resources/emerging-technologies-utilities-future-keep-eye/

## 8: High-Tech Healthcare

1     Details available at Accenture, 'Digital Adoption: Reaction or Revolution?', 6 August 2021, https://www.accenture.com/us-en/insights/health/digital-adoption-healthcare-reaction-or-revolution

2     Susan Ladika, 'Bumps in the Road Ahead for Retail Health', MHE publication,17 January 2022,https://www.managedhealthcareexecutive.com/view/bumps-in-the-road-ahead-for-retail-health

3     Details available at Cognizant, 'Healthcare on Demand: New Provider Business Models for the Digital Economy', https://www.cognizant.com/us/en/whitepapers/documents/new-provider-business-models-for-the-digital-economy-codex4969.pdf

4    Hari Pulakkat, 'SMAC: Combining Technologies Is the Next Big Infotech Revolution', 28 December 2013, https://economictimes. indiatimes.com/tech/internet/smac-combining-technologies-is-the-next-big-infotech-revolution/articleshow/28024401.cms

5    Details available at McKinsey and Company, 'The Essentials of Healthcare Innovation', 5 May 2021, https://www.mckinsey.com/ business-functions/strategy-and-corporate-finance/our-insights/the-essentials-of-healthcare-innovation

6    Details available at Bernard Marr, 'The Five Biggest Healthcare Tech Trends in 2022', Forbes, 10 January 2022, https://www.forbes.com/ sites/bernardmarr/2022/01/10/the-five-biggest-healthcare-tech-trends-in-2022/?sh=2f9c22c654d0

7    'A Virtual ER', *Pittsburg Post-Gazette*, https://www.post-gazette. com/news/health/2021/12/20/televisit-pilot-program-Center-for-Emergency-Medicine-UPMC-Bureau-of-Emergency-Medical-Services/stories/202112170142

8    Details available at StartUs, 'Discover the Top 10 Healthcare Industry Trends and Innovations in 2023', https://www.startus-insights.com/ innovators-guide/top-10-healthcare-industry-trends-innovations-in-2021/

9    Details available at Anthony Capone, 'The Future Of Healthcare Technology', 11 January 2022, https://www.forbes.com/sites/ forbestechcouncil/2022/01/11/the-future-of-healthcare-technology/?sh=5d0478b94750

10    Details available at Mike Miliard, 'CISOs See Opportunities Amid Heightened Cybersecurity Risks', 14 March 2022, https:// www.healthcareitnews.com/news/cisos-see-opportunities-amid-heightened-cybersecurity-risks

11    Chuck Appleby et al., 'Digital Transformation', Deloitte, 26 October 2021, https://www2.deloitte.com/us/en/insights/industry/health-care/digital-transformation-in-healthcare.html

12    Details available at World Economic Forum, 'If Healthcare Doesn't Strengthen Its Cybersecurity, It Could Soon Be in Critical Condition', 8 November 2021, https://www.weforum.org/agenda/2021/11/ healthcare-cybersecurity/

13    https://www.researchgate.net/publication/366598760_An_ intelligent_non-invasive_system_for_automated_diagnosis_of_ anemia_exploiting_a_novel_dataset

14    https://www.youtube.com/watch?v=IUoZQyGgcrg

## 9: Weapons of Mass Disruption

1   Details available at Qureca, 'Overview on Quantum Initiatives Worldwide—Update Mid 2021', 19 July 2021, https://www.qureca.com/overview-on-quantum-initiatives-worldwide-update-mid-2021/

2   Gil Press, 'New Funding for Quantum Computing Accelerates Worldwide', *Forbes*, 31 January 2023, https://www.forbes.com/sites/gilpress/2023/01/31/new-funding-for-quantum-computing-accelerates-worldwide/?sh=5de92978b35b

3   Details available at NTRS–NASA Technical Report Server, 'Digital Twins and Living Models at NASA', https://ntrs.nasa.gov/citations/20210023699

## Epilogue

1   Pranjal Sharma, 'Can Help Indian Govt Replicate Digital Public Goods in Other EMs: IBM CEO', *Business Standard*, 21 January 2023, https://www.business-standard.com/article/companies/hopeful-that-we-re-reaching-the-end-of-licence-raj-ibm-s-ceo-krishna-123011801310_1.html

2   Pranjal Sharma, 'We'll Work with Indian Organisations on Online Safety: Julie Inman Grant', *Business Standard*, 20 January 2023, https://www.business-standard.com/article/companies/we-ll-work-with-indian-organisations-on-online-safety-julie-inman-grant-123011901329_1.html

3   Inderpal Bhandari, 'Creating a Global Ecosystem for the Quantum Industry', 22 December 2021, https://www.ibm.com/blogs/journey-to-ai/2021/12/creating-a-global-ecosystem-for-the-quantum-industry/

4   World Economic Forum, 'What Is Stakeholder Capitalism?', https://www.weforum.org/agenda/2021/01/klaus-schwab-on-what-is-stakeholder-capitalism-history-relevance/ For tech businesses, people and planet will have to be priorities, not just profits.

# Index

AB InBev, 50

Accelerated Processing Unit (APU), 167

Accenture, 10, 53, 135

accident-prevention systems, 97, see also safety; Safety Innovations in Intelligent Mobility

accountability, x–xi, 106, 151, 160–161

adaptive cruise control (ACC), 90–91

additive manufacturing, xxxviii, xlvii, 3–4, 33, 57, 59, 86

adhesives: bio-based, xxvi, 53; in healthcare, 54; recyclable, xxvi, 53; renewable, xxvi, 53; solventless, xxvi, 53; sustainable, xxvi, 53; tapes, 174; waterborne, xxvi, 53

advanced air mobility (AAM), 9–13

advanced analytics. See big data analytics

advanced driver assistance systems, xlvii, 83

advanced genome characterization techniques, xxxiii, 32

advanced military capabilities, xxxix, 9, 15–17, see also Aerodefence technologies

advanced therapy medicinal products (ATMPs), xxxvii, 147

aerial refueling, 16
aerial ride-sharing companies, 11
Aero-defence technologies, 15
Aerofarm, 30
aeroponic methods, 30
aerospace, xxxviii, xli, 4, 9–10, 15,
    19, 22, 51, 54–55, 57, 169; and
    defence, xxxviii, 19, 55, 57;
    industry, 21, 57
Agility Prime, 15
agricultural: biotechnology, 31;
    technology, 26
agricultural sector, 26, 70;
    population growth and, 25
agriculture, xxxii, 5, 23, 26, 28–29,
    31–32, 50, 145; drones in, 24;
    and food supply chain market,
    27
agrigenomics, xxxii
agri-mechanization, 24
Airbus, xxxi, xxxviii, 12, 14, 16,
    55, 102
Aircraft and auto manufacturers,
    xxxi, 57; 3D printing and, 57
air-to-air refueling. See aerial
    refueling
AkzoNobel's big data service
    Intertrac Vision, 46
Alexa, xiv
Alliance of Automobile
    Manufacturers, 85
Alternate Fuels, 12
Amazon, 20; Prime Air drone
    programme, 21
Ampaire, xxxviii, 14
AMR, 74
analytics, xxv, 108, 114, 129

Aptiv, 78
aquaponics, 30
Argo AI, 91
Arianespace SA (France), 5
artificial general intelligence (AGI),
    xv
artificial intelligence (AI), xxiv,
    xxxviii, xlvi, 1, 3, 17–19,
    26, 28–29, 63, 65, 110–111,
    113–114, 136, 138; algorithms,
    37, 146, 161, 166; based energy
    management solutions, xx;
    based solutions, 140–141;
    based technology, 35, 151;
    chatbot, xii; Chipsets, xl, xliii,
    74–75; driven flavours, xxxiv;
    in genomics, xxxv, 144, 146–
    147; inspired ML methods, 147;
    in medical diagnostics market,
    140; in medical imaging, 138;
    for NGS analysis, 144; powered
    Data Lake, 98; powered robots
    (see cobots under robots);
    powered smart grids, 132
Association of American Medical
    Colleges, US, 140
Association of Global Automakers,
    85
Audi, 91, 93, 95, 159
augmented reality (AR), xxxviii,
    xlii, 3, 9, 82, 84, 86, 88, 157,
    165, 170–171
Augury, 65
Autoimmune diseases, xxxvi, 146
automakers, xlvii, 80, 83
automated guided vehicles (AGVs),
    xl, xlii, 39, 72–74, 92

automated storage and retrieval
  systems (ASRS), 39
automatic: air-to-air refuelling,
  16; driverless technology,
  80; inspection and testing, 4;
  transportation systems, 79
automation, xii, xv–xvii, 39–40,
  66, 68, 72–73, 79, 86, 107, 118,
  128; economy, xii; Shukla on,
  xvii
automotive industry, xliv, xlvii,
  54, 64, 79–80, 82–83, 85–87, 96
autonomous: driving, xliv, 91,
  158; flight systems, 21; ride-
  sharing, 89–94; shared mobility
  services, 89; technologies, xli,
  92; vehicles (AVs), xliii, 79, 81,
  89, 91–95, 165; vehicle delivery
  service, 92
aviation fuel, xxxviii, 14;
  alternative, 12
aviation industry, xxxviii, 13–14;
  decarbonization and, 12

backplanes, xxv, 47
Badawi, Ramsey, 141
banking, financial services and
  insurance (BFSI), 162–163
barcoding, 39
batteries, xxv, 11, 47, 73, 84,
  119, 161; advanced lead-
  acid, 124; flow, xxiv, 66,
  124–125; flywheel, xxiv, 124;
  High-energy density, 14; in
  industries, 66; lithium-ion,
  xxiv, xxviii, 66–67, 124–125;
  nickel-iron, xxiv; nickel-

cadmium, xxiv; recyclable,
  xx; swapping, xlvi, 84;
  sodium-based, xxiv, 66, 124;
  technologies, xxix, 16, 66–67,
  84, 125
battery energy storage system
  (BESS), 124
Beck, Jeff, 39
Beckham, David, 111
bee-based natural pollination
  cycle, 23
beeswax, xxvi, 53
BESS market, 124–125
Bezos, Jeff, 4
big data: analytics, xxxviii,
  3–4, 18, 46, 63, 86, 118;
  technologies, 144
bike-sharing, xli
bin Salman, Mohammed, 92
bio-based: alternatives, xxvi,
  49; packaging materials, 45;
  personal hygiene and beauty
  products, 45; plastics, xxvi,
  48–49, 53
bioceramics, xxvii, 58
biodegradable/recyclable plastics,
  xxv
biologics, xxxvii, 148
biomedical engineering
  techniques, xxxvii, 148
biometrics, 10, 115, 175;
  advanced voice authentication
  technology, 104
biomolecules, 32
bio-plastics. See bio-based
  plastics
biotechnology, 154

blockchain, xxiv, xxvi, xxix,
    xxxii, xxxiv, xxxviii, 26–27,
    29, 38, 40, 46, 48, 127–128,
    157–158; based enterprises,
    128; farming, 27; in supply
    chains, xxxiv; technology, 47,
    128–129
Blue Origin Federation, 4–5
Blue River Technology, 28
BMW, 87, 90–91, 93
Boeing, xxxi, 55, 102; 777X, 57,
    see also Airbus
border security, countering, 18
bring your own device (BYOD),
    107, 166
Burnstein, Jeff, 72
business: leaders, ix, xii, xvii, 60,
    98, 172; models, xi–xii, xiv, 21,
    29, 97, 115, 119, 126, 132–133,
    171, 176

CaaS, xliv, 79
camera technology, 1; artificial
    intelligent in, 5; Light
    Detection and Ranging, 29
cancer, xxiii, xxxvi, 141, 143–147,
    149
Cape Air, 14
Capgemini, 85
Capone, Anthony, 151
car-as-a-service (CaaS), xliv
carbon capture and utilization
    technologies, xxiii–xxiv, 124
carbon capture utilization and
    storage (CCUS), xx, xxiv,
    123–124
carbon footprint, 9, 44–45, 47, 49

care-delivery business models,
    135
carjacking, 81–82
cars, autonomous self-driving,
    82, 89–91, 94; hacking,
    81–82; sharing, xli, 87, see also
    autonomous, shared mobility
CDI Energy Products, 57
cellular networks, xl, 6, 95
Center for Strategic and
    International Studies, 114
Centrica, London, 116
ceramics, 43–44, see also
    bioceramics
ChargeX, 88
charging pads, xli, 68–69
chatbots, xii, xvi; healthcare, xiv
ChatGPT, xiii–xiv
CH-Bioforce, Finnish startup 50
chemical industry, xx, xxv, 44,
    47–48, 52, 121
chemicals and materials sector,
    xxv
Chemistry 4.0, 47–49
Cherry, Simon, 141
chlorosilanes, xxv, 47
choose your own device (CYOD),
    107
civil society, 22, 156, 160
clean energy infrastructure, 117,
    see also modern green house
    practices
climate change, xi, 42, 117, 132
cloud computing, 18–19, 46, 48,
    76, 104, 107, 129, 151, 159,
    164–167; Distributed Denial of
    Service [DDoS] of, 165

cloud-based solutions, 142, 164; mobile and, 46

clustered regularly interspaced short palindromic repeats (CRISPR), xxxv, 145; Cas9, xxxi, 145

$CO_2$ emissions, xxiv, 46, 52, 63, 123; from defence industry, 9

Cognizant, xv–xvi, 152

Colgate-Palmolive, 65

collaborative robots. See cobots under robots

company owned/business only (COBO), 107

company owned/personally enabled (COPE), 107

composites, xxv, xxvii, 47, 54–56, 60

compound annual growth rate (CAGR), xxxi, xl, xliii, 37–38, 53–54, 56, 64–66, 68–69, 72–73, 80–82, 105–106, 108, 120–121, 124–125, 146–147, 162–163, 171

connected vehicles, xl–xli, 96

construction industry, 51

consumer preferences, xi–xii, xxix, 34, 36–38, 44

consumer-to-business (C2B), 136, healthcare, 135

contactless solutions, 41

cooperative driving, extended electronic (NLOS) vision, xlii, 74

cordless tools, xl, 67

Cota technology, 69

COVID-19 pandemic, 8, 26, 40, 75, 86, 97, 135, 137, 152–153; related research, 158

creative destruction, xi, 174

Cruise by GM, 93

cryogenic storage, xxxix, 13

customer care, xv

cyber thievery, 81

cyber-attacks, xxv, 113, 130

cybersecurity, xl–xli, 40, 81, 105–109, 114–115, 152, 160, 163

Daimler, 87, 90, 93

dairy alternative sector, 37

data: analytics, xxxviii, 9, 46, 151, (see also big data analytics); localization, 164; privacy, xli; science, 40, 113; transfer, xxv, 47, 102

Data Lake, 99

data management, master 18; Real-time, 148

decarbonization, xx, xxiii, xxv, 9, 13, 44, 120, 130; in Singapore, 131, see also zero-emission sistem

decentralized identity, 156–157, see also digital identity-based system

decision intelligence, 156, 158–159

Decker, Erik, 152

deep fakes, 110–113

DeepMind (AI), xiv

defence industry, xxxviii, xli, 4, 9, 17, 22, 169

Defense Advanced Research Projects Agency, 19

dendritic cell therapy, 148

DevOps, 107

diagnostic imaging, xxxv, 138; AI in, xxxv, see also teleradiology

digital battlefield: devices, xxxix, 17–19; global market analysis, 18; products and systems, 17–19

digital: farming, xxxii; healthcare, 136; identity-based system, 175; innovations, 38, 41–42, 79; manufacturing operations, xlii, 85; public infrastructure, x; technologies, xi, xxvi, 46, 48–49, 126, 135, 150, 153; thread, 3, 9; transformation, 65, 151–152; twin technology, xli, 18, 86, 155, 158, 168–172; wallet IDs, 175–176

Digital Tapestry, Lockheed Martin, 4

digitization/digitalization, xxxv, 9, 39, 46, 48, 126–127, 131, 139, 153, 166

DNA analysis, 32, 145–146, 156, 158

Douglas Insights, 7

driverless transportation-as-a-service offerings, 87

drones, xxx, xxxii, xxxix, xl, xlii, 16–17, 19–24, 28–29, 47, 67, 71, 113–114, 159; deliveries, 20–21; in factories, 70–71; as farmer's tool, 24; Hendrickson on, 21; inspection, 21; self-piloted, 132

Drone Shakti programme, 24

drug discovery, xxxv, 144–145, 161

Drug Supply Chain Security Act (2013), 38

D-wave, 162

dynamic optimization, xlii, 168

Earth Observation, 6

edge AI, xliii, 76, 166–167

edge computing, 40, 64, 101, 159, 165–167

Edge IoT, 167

Electra.aero, Inc., 16

Electric Aircrafts, xx, 13–14

electrical: and electronics industry, 54; grid infrastructure, xxv, 129; flying cars/vehicles, 10, 15, 83, (see also electric vehicles (EVs); ships, xx

electricity, xxix, xxxix, 16, 22, 128–131, see also electrification

Electric short take-off and landing aircraft (eSTOLs), xxxix, 16

electric vehicles (EVs), xv, xxiv, xxviii, xxx, xliii, xliv, xlvi, 79, 81, 83–84, 92, 98, 119, 131

electric vertical take-off and landing aircraft (eVTOLs), 11, 14–15

electrification, xxx, xlvi, 9, 83, 87; of aircraft, xxxviii, 13

electronic: aircraft technologies, 13; consumer, 6, 66–68; warfare systems, xxxix, 17

electronic health records (EHRs), 136, 139

End-to-End Automotive Platforms,
xlii, 83
end-use industries, xxiii, xxvi,
51–52, 55–57
energy: consumption, xi, 63, 131;
sector, xxii, 117, 119, 126,
128–129, 133; storage, xx, xxii,
xxiv, 119, 124, 130; transition,
xxiii, see also fuel
energy as a service (EaaS), 127
Energy Landscape, technologies
defining, 127–129
engineering, 43, 72, 99, 146, 148,
160
Enhanced Oil Recovery (EOR),
xxiv
entrepreneurship, 6
environment, social and
governance (ESG), x–xi
Environmental Protection Agency,
44
environmental sustainability, x,
25, 63
eSolutech (Brazil), 92
ethical hackers, 111
ethics, x–xi
eukaryotic genome, xxxvi, 145
Eurecat Centre, xlii
European Green Deal, Europe, 38
European Space Agency (ESA), 6,
101
Everett, Robinson O., 154
Evertree, French startup, xxx, 49
EV fluids, xxv
Eviation, xxxiv, 14
extended detection and response
(XDR), 105

extended reality (XR), 157

fake information, 111
Falsified Medicines Directive,
USA, 38
Farahany, Nita A., 154
FASTag, 99–100
Faury, Guillaume, 8
FCVs, 55
Federal Communications
Commission (FCC), 7, 70
Federal Information Security
Management Act (FISMA), 106
fiberoptic properties, xxv, 47
Fifth Industrial Revolution (5IR),
ix–xi, xv, 62, 133, 174
first mile/last mile (FM/LM)
problem, 94
Fit Analytics, Berlin, 109
food and agriculture sector, xxvii,
25–26
Food Safety Modernization Act
(2011), 38
food storage and transportation,
38–40
food-tech, xxvii, xxix
Ford Motor Company, 89, 91,
93–95
forensics, xxxvi, 145
fossil carbon, xxvi, 49
fossil fuels, xxvi, 13, 45, 82,
121–122, 133; based industrial
chemicals, 49; combustion
sources, 123
fourth industrial revolution
(Industry 4.0), ix, xi, xxv, 23,
33, 47, 62–65, 71, 76, 169

fifth industrial revolution
(Industry 5.0), ix–xi, xv, 62,
83, 71, 133, 174
5G Network, 18–19, 85, 97, 100–
105, 115, 136, 157, 162, see also
6G Network
fuel: cells, xx, xxxvii, 12–13,
121; hydrogen-based aviation,
xxxviii; efficiency, xxxv, 13,
22, 46, see also fossil fuels
fully autonomous car, xl, 95
functional genomics sector, xxxiii,
31
future air mobility (FAM), 10

garments and textiles industry,
109–110
Gastrograph AI, 36
gate-keeping activity, 175
GE Aviation, 57
gene-based innovations, 135
gene: editing, xxxv, xxxvi, 145,
155; therapies, xxiii, xxxv,
xxxvi, 147–149
General Data Protection Regulation
(GDPR), 106
General Motors-GM (US), xl, 83,
89–90, 93
generative artificial intelligence,
156, 158–159
genomics, xxxvi, 33, 143–146;
integration of AI in, xxxvi,
146–147
gesture-tracking devices, 171
glass fibre composites, xxvi, 56
global electricity production, 131
Global Lighthouse Network, 62–63

global manufacturing sector, 65
global mobility ecosystem, xliv,
79
global positioning system, 29, 159
Globalstar, 7
global warming, 9, 117
google, xiii–xiv; Tensor Processing
Unit (TPU) of, 167
governance, ix–xi, xxxiv, 38,
107–108
Grant, Julie Inman, 176
graphics processing units (GPUs),
166
green: ammonia, xx, 122;
chemicals, xxv; chemistry/
sustainable chemistry, 44–48;
hydrogen, xi, xx, xxiii, 119–
122; jeans, 45; pesticides, xi
Green Ultimate, xxvi, 49
grid-interactive efficient buildings
(GEBs), 131
GSM Association (GSMA),
103–104

hackers, 81–82, 108, see also
ethical hackers
Hailo, Israel, 76
*Harnessing AI to Accelerate Energy
Transition*, WEF report, 117
healthcare, xxx, 54, 57–58, 68,
75, 103, 134–139, 151–152,
169–171, 173; access to, x;
biomarkers, 143; cell therapies,
xxxvii, 148–149; cloud-based
solutions, 142; consumers, 135;
ECG sensor, 153; EEG sensors,
153; magnetic resonance

imaging (MRI), xxxv, 142;
somatic cell therapy medicinal
products, xxxvii, 147;
technology adoption, 136–138,
151; total-body scanner, 141
healthcare industry, xiii, 54,
135–136, 138–141, 146, 151,
162; bioceramic material in, 58
Health Information Technology for
Economic and Clinical Health
(HITECH) Act, US, 139
Health Insurance Portability and
Accountability Act (HIPAA),
106, 151
Hendrickson, Calsee, 21
Heraclitus, 173
high-performance computing
(HPC), 144
high-performance electric motors,
14
highways, 98–100
Hindustan Unilever Limited (HUL),
Dapada, 63–64
Hoke, Dirk, 11
holoportation, 101
Honda, 90–91, 94
Hour One, Tel Aviv, 111
human-like response, xiii
human-machine collaboration, 18
human-to-PC screen interface, 157
hydrogen, 12, 116, 120, 122; based
aviation fuel, xxxviii, 13;
powered aircraft, xxxix, 13
hydroponic technology, 30
hydroxyapatite, xxxii, 58
Hyundai, 11, 78, 90–91, 93
Hyundai IONIQ, 78

IBM, 35, 108, 161–162, 174; AI
platform Watson, 35
ICEYE (Finland), 6
IDTechEx report, 29
Illumina, USA, 145
image processing, xxxix, 16, 28;
with artificial intelligence, 28
Immersive Technologies, 150,
156–157
Indian Council of Agriculture
Research, 24
Indian Institute of Food Processing
Technology (IIFPT), 33
Indian Space Research
Organization, 5–6
industrial chemicals, fossil fuel–
based, xxvi
industrial internet of things (IIoT),
46, 63–64, 165, 169
information and communication
technology (ICT), 129
Inmarsat, 7
innovations, xxxviii, 5, 24, 29,
44, 49–50, 70, 77, 96, 135, 138;
technologies, 9–10, 66, 83, 126
In-Q-Tel, 114
Insights, Douglas, 7
Institute of Engineering and
Technology, 156
Integrated: computer vision,
xxxviii, 3; data sharing, 151;
marine automation system, 17
Intel, 11
intelligence communities, 113–
114
intelligent process automation
(IPA), xv; based chatbot, xv–

xvii; tractor-pull implements, 29
International Air Travel Association (IATA), 175
International Civil Aviation Organization (ICAO), 175
International Co-operation for Animal Research Using Space (ICARUS), 5
International Space Station, 5, 101
internet of medical Internet of medical things (IoMT), 136–137
internet of things (IoT), xxiv–xxv, xxvii, xxxii, xxxix, xl, 6–7, 10, 17–19, 26–27, 29, 48, 62–63, 102–104, 129, 165, 168; and edge devices, 166; in energy market, 127–128
Intvo, 87–88
Iridium, 7
IT/OT convergence, 107

Jassy, Andy, 113
jet engine, 43, 58; GE9X, 57
Joby Aviation, 15
Johnston, Cesar, 70
Jovic, Marija, 45
just-in-time (JIT), xlii, 73

knowledge-based processes, xvi
Krishi Vigyan Kendras (KVK), 24
Krishna, Arvind, 174
Kurlas, Robin, 72

laboratories, xxxvii, 149; digitalization, 150
labour shortages, 30, 40

lasers, 15, 41
launch vehicles, reusable, 2
LEED, green building programmes, 52
The Lift HEXA, 15
lightweighting materials, 54–55
livestock farming sector, 26, 33
low-cost technologies, 59
Lucid Motors, California, 92
luxury car segment, 56
Lyft, 93–95

machine learning (ML), xiv, 2, 28–29, 40, 48–49, 63, 85, 109–110, 127, 136, 162–163
MagniX, xxxviii, 14
market: AI in genomics, 147; autonomous train, 80; battery, 66, 125; BESS, 124–125; CCUS, xx, xxiv, 123–124; cloud security, 108; composites, 55; cybersecurity, 106; global adhesive tape, 54; global agri-genomics, 31; global AI chipsets, xliii, 76; global automotive cybersecurity, 81; global biodegradable plastics, xxvi, 53; global blockchain, 128; global cell and gene therapy, 149; global cloud security, 108; global digital battlefield, xxxix; global digital healthcare, 152; global edge computing, 166; global lightweighting material, xxxi, 56; global smart manufacturing, 64; lightweighting material,

xxxi, 56; material, 54–55, 58; microgrid, xxviii, 130; NGS, 144–145; quantum computing software, 162–163; Satellite IoT, 7; 3D printing material, 57; wireless charging, 68–69

Martin, Lockheed, 4

mass customization, 36, 57–59, 74, 109

materials industry, xxxi

McCormick, 35–36

McKinsey Center for Advanced Connectivity, 29

McKinsey Global Institute, 29

Meagher, Thomas, Lt. col., 15

Medica Group (UK), 142

medical care, xxxvi; AI in, 146, see also healthcare

Medium-density fibreboard (MDF), 52

Mehra, Aashish, xlvii

Mercedes-Benz, 90, 161

metals, 43, 57–59, 67

Metals Group Australia, 92

metaverse, 101–102, 156–157

military devices, xxxv, 17, 19

mobility-as-a-service (Maas), xxxix, 79, 127

modern greenhouse practice, 25

molecular marker-assisted crop breeding, xliv, 31

Moley Robotic Kitchen, Britain, 34

Moon and Mars explorations, 5

Motional, 78–79; Level 4 Avs, 79; robotaxi service, 78

mtDNA, 146

Müller, Andreas, 102

multimodal imaging, 138, 141

Musk, Elon, 7, 123

Nandlall, Vish, 167

National Aeronautics and Space Administration (NASA), xli, 33, 101–102, 169

National Food Security Strategy 2051, 41

National Highway Authority of India (NHAI), 98–99

National Highway Traffic Safety Administration (NHTSA), 89

National Institutes of Food Technology, Entrepreneurship and Management, 34

National Mission on Quantum Technologies and Applications, 160

National Security Commission on Artificial Intelligence (NSCAI), US, 113

natural fibre composites, xxxi, 56

natural language processing (NLP), xx, 136

near-field communication (NFC), xli, 69

Nervana, Intel, 167

net-zero emission goals, xxviii, xxxviii, 9

new aircraft programmes, xxxi, 55, see also Electric Aircrafts; electronic aircraft technologies

New Shepard suborbital rocket system, 4

New Space Economy, 5–8

next-generation sequencing (NGS), xxxvi, 143–145
NFT/Tokenization, see non-fungible token (NFTs)
NGVs, 55
nickel-metal hydride, xxix, 124
Nissan (Japan), xl, 87, 89, 91, 93
non-fungible token (NFTs), 156–158
NoTraffic, 88
Novel Drone Applications, 19–20
Nvidia, 76

Olson, Gregory, 43
on-demand air taxis, 11
One ID, 175
Ontario Smart Grid Fund, 130
OpenAI, ChatGPT of, xiv
operational technology (OT), 107
Optimus, 61
OrbComm, 7
order-picking technologies, 39
original equipment manufacturers (OEMs), xl, 13, 56, 82, 84, 86–87, 89–92, 94
Ossia Inc, 69
over-the-air wireless charging, xli, 69–70
oxo-degradable, 53

paints and coatings, 50–51
Palmer, Megan J., 154
Pang, Edward, 43
parallel sequencing technologies, xxxiii, 31
passports, 174–176

Patange, Aniket, 117
Payment Card Industry Data Security Standard (PCI-DSS), 106
pharmaceuticals, xxxvii, 63, 148
Philips Healthcare, 142
phone hacking, 114
Photonics, 74
Planet Labs, Inc. (US), 6
plant-based: alternatives, xxvii; meat and dairy, xxxiii, 37–38; surfactants, xxx, 49–50
plastics, xxiv, xxx, xxxi, 47, 53, 57, 59; biodegradable, xxvi; high-performance, xxxi, 57–58; single-use, xxvi, 53
Polyetheretherketone (PEEK), 58
powder coatings technology, 51–52, see also paints and coatings
power generation, 119–120, 125, 133
pressurized hot water extraction (PHWE), 50
privatization, 6
process automation, x, xvii, 97, see also intelligent process automation (IPA); robotic process automation (RPA)
Production Linked Incentive, 24
propulsion systems, xxxix, 13

quantum computing, 159–163, 172
Quantum Computing Governance Principles, 160

radio frequency (RF), xxxvi, 69
Radio Frequency Identification (RFID), 39, 92, 99, 115

Radmol AI, 151
Raggio, Tony, 73
R&D, 31, 49, 138
regenerative medicine, xxxv,
    xxxvii, 148
Regional and Remote Communities
    Reliability Fund, 130
remote monitoring, 31, 134
remote sensing, xxvii, 26
Renault, 87
renewable energy sources, xxiii,
    131
RescapeInnovation, 150
resins: petro-sourced, xxvi, 49;
    urea-formaldehyde, xxvi, 49
Reuter, While Florian, 10
revenue-generating model, xii
ride-hailing services, xli, 11, 87,
    89, 95
Rivest-Shamir-Adleman (RSA), 163
RNA, 146, 148
RoboChef, Chennai, 35
robotaxi, 78–79, 89, 94
robotic process automation (RPA),
    xv–xvi, 18
robotics/robots, xvi, xxxii,
    xxxviii, 3, 10, 15, 28–29,
    34–35, 40, 49, 61–63, 71,
    85, 138; chef, 41; cobots or
    collaborative, xl, xlii, 71–72,
    85; cylindrical, 61; farm, xxxii,
    27; human, 61; industrial, xliii,
    41, 65, 71; kitchens, xxxiv, 34;
    microbots, 137–138; mobile,
    xl, 67; nursing, 137; small
    autonomous, 29
Rockefeller Foundation, 42

RUSBoost algorithm, 154

safety, 12, 18, 21–22, 68, 71, 80,
    85, 88, 95, 112, 115, 176
Safety Innovations in Intelligent
    Mobility, 84–85
Saran, Samir, x
SARS-Cov2 virus, 153
satellite(s), xxxiii, 1–2, 5–8, 22;
    communications, 156, 159–163;
    IoT, 7; miniaturization of,
    xxxviii, 1; visuals, 114
Schmidt, Eric, 113
Schneider Electric, Hyderabad, 63
Schuh, Christopher, 43
search engines, xiii–xv; business
    model, xiv
SEAT S.A., xlii, 70
secure access service edge (SASE),
    105
secure sockets layer/transport layer
    security (SSL/TLS), 163
security orchestration, automation
    and response (SOAR), 105
self-driving: abilities, xlii, 83; cars/
    vehicles, 81, 89–90, 92–93,
    see also cars, autonomous self
    driving
semiautonomous cars/vehicles,
    89–92
semiconductors, 74–75, 80–81
Sensor-embedded smart roads, 98
sensor fusion technology, 16
Shape-Memory Material, 43
Shapeways, New York, 110
shared: mobility, xxxviii, xliii,
    86–88; transportation, xli

Shukla, Mihir, xiii
Silicon Valley, 8
siloed methodologies, xxxvii, 150
Singh, Gurpreet, 135
Sironix Renewables, 50
6G Network, 97, 115, 157
Skyline restaurant, Fairfield, 72
Skylo, 8
small satellite constellations, 2, 5,
    7–8
smart: devices, xxv, 68, 129;
    factories, xl, xlii, 9, 63, 85,
    124; farming, 26–27; grids, xx,
    xxiii, 129–130; logistics, 38;
    manufacturing, xl, xlvii, 62,
    71, 76, 85, 169; sensors, 18;
    transmission and distribution,
    xxii, xxv, 120, 129; vehicles,
    98, 100
smartphones, xxv, 47, 68, 84, 95
social, mobile, analytics and cloud
    (SMAC), 136
social inclusion, x–xi, 174
Society of Automotive Engineers
    (SAE), 89–90
software composition analysis
    (SCA), 107
software-defined perimeter (SDP),
    107
space: exploration technologies,
    xxxiii, 3, 5; industry, xxxiii, 1,
    6; travel, 2; tourism 5
SpaceX (US), 7
Sparrow chatbot, xiv–xv
Spices Board India, 42
Spire Global, Inc. (US), 6
Spoonshot, 36

Sprinkling of Artificial Intelligence
    Flavours, 35
Stafford, Alexander, 116
startups, xxvi, 1, 3, 13, 35, 49–50,
    87–88, 93, 112, 114, 151
StartUs Insights, 87
stingray tracking devices, 115
stock keeping unit (SKU), 38
Suborbital space flights, 4
substrates, xxv, 47, 54
supercomputers, xlii, 83, 159, 162
Supernal, US, 11
supply chains, xxxiv, 27, 31, 33,
    38, 40, 47, 62, 65, 79, 86–87
sustainability, xxx, xxxviii, xxxix,
    13, 40, 44–46, 63–64, 82, 87,
    119–120
sustainable: air mobility, 8–10;
    alternatives, xxvi, 49; aviation,
    xxxviii, 12–14; bio-lubricants,
    xxv; development goals, x–xi;
    manufacturing, xi
sustainable fuels (SAF), xxxviii, 13
Swarm Technologies, 7
Synthace, 49
Synthesia, US, 111
synthesize surfactants, 50, see also
    plant-based surfactants
synthetic media industry, 112

tablets, xxx, 47, 68–69, see also
    smartphones
Taylor, Dylan, 4
T-Cell therapy, 148, see also
    Advanced therapy medicinal
    products (ATMPs); dendritic
    cell therapy; vivo viral vector-

based therapy (Zolgensma, Luxturna)
Tech-Enhanced Kitchens, 33, see also chef robots under robots
technological advancements, x, xxiii, xxv, xxviii, 13, 44, 52, 129, 141, 174
technology companies, xx, 95, 137
telehealth, 136–137
teleradiology, xxxv, 138, 141–143
Teleradiology Solutions (Telradsol) (US), 142
Tesla, xl, 61, 90, 94–95
Tesla Optimus, 62
Thales, France, 104
thermal energy storage (TES), 125
thermal scanners, 41
thermochemical storage (TCS), 125
thermoplastics, high-performance, xxvii, 57
3D imaging services, 142
3D modelling, 4
3D printing, xxxi, xxxii, xxxviii, 3, 18, 34, 49, 86, 110; consumer goods, 59; in Food, xxix, 33–34; mass customization in, 58; and materials, 57–60
3D report viewing, xxxv, 142
3D scanning, 109
3D technologies, 110
tissue-engineered medicines, 147–148, see also T-Cell therapy
Toyota, 89, 91, 93–94
transparency, xv, 27, 40, 47, 112, 128, 136, 151, 174
transparent conductors, xxv, 47

tricalcium phosphate, xxvii, 58
Trivedi, Parth, 8
Trudeau, Justin, 160

Uber, 78–79, 93–95
UI/UX (user interface and user experience), 88
ultra-classic airbags, 82
UNDP Accelerator Lab India, 41
United States Innovation and Competition Act (USICA), 75
unmanned aerial vehicles (UAVs), x, 14, 19, 22, 28, (see also drones; space tourism); rotary-wing, 22; fixed-wing, 22; small, 29
Urban air mobility, xxxviii, 12
USARDA Holdings (US), 142

vehicle intelligence platform (VIP), 83
vehicles: onboard infotainment, xlii, 83; onboard sensors, xliv, 79
vehicle-to-cloud (V2C), 95
Vehicle-to-everything (V2X), xxxviii, xl, 74, 85, 95
vehicle-to-infrastructure (V2I), xl, 73, 95
vehicle-to-network (V2N) connectivity, 73
vehicle-to-pedestrian (V2P), 95
vehicle-to-vehicle (V2V), xli, 73, 95–96
Vera Rubin Observatory, Chile, 2
vertical farming, xxxii, 25, 29–31
veterinary sciences, 145
Virgin Galactic, 3, 5

virtual automotive purchase
process, 88
virtual ER, 137
virtual reality (VR), 4, 9, 18,
101, 103, 136, 157, 159, 165,
170; devices, 171; distraction
therapy, 150
visual tracking algorithms, xxxix,
16
Vitaldini, Grazia, 12
Viveros, Marisa, 108
vivo viral vector-based therapy
(Zolgensma, Luxturna), 147
Vodafone IoT, 7
voice recognition technologies, xiv,
xviii, 3
volatile organic compound (VOC),
51–52
Volkswagen, 89
Volkswagen AG, 90
Volocopter, 11
voluntary data sharing, 113
Volvo (Sweden), xl
VPN technology, 106

WAIR, California, 110
Walmart, 20, 91; drone-delivery
programme, 20

warehouses: automated, xxxiv;
Hybrid semiautomated system,
39; management system, 39
Watson, IBM, 35
Waymo of Alphabet, xliv, 87, 91,
94–95
wearables, 10, 134
Whitesides, George, 3
Wiegand, Daniel, 10
Wi-Fi 6, 103, 115
wireless charging, xl, xli, xlvi,
67–70, 84
wireless charging, xl, xli, xlvi,
67–68; over-the-air 69–70;
technology, NFC, xli, 69; Radio
Frequency 70
wireless LAN controller (WLC),
69
Work, Robert, 113
World Economic Forum (WEF), 3,
62–63, 117–118, 154, 160
Woven Planet, by Toyota, 93

ZeroAvia, 12
zero-emission system, 12
zero trust, 105
zirconium, 58
Zymergen, 49

# A Special Thank You

The MarketsandMarkets Research team contributed generously with their reports as a support for me, as a knowledge partner. I would like to thank the team members who worked on the sectoral reports:

- Rajiv Kalia, Dipak Mahajan, Vijender Agarwal, Shraddha Shrivastava for healthcare
- Lakshmi Narayanan, Pradeep Srivastava, Neeraj Verma, Kaushik Singh for chemicals and materials
- Balaji Sreedhar, Shekeb Naim, Sameer Bhatnagar for technology
- Apurva Agarwal, Tanuj Goyal for advanced manufacturing and semiconductors

- Syed Hayat Rizvi for food and beverage, and agriculture
- Ashish Bhadola for energy and power
- Vaibhav Dixit for aerospace
- Navin Rajendra for automotive

# Acknowledgements

The idea of *The Next New* germinated during the COVID pandemic. A global emergency brought technologists, scientists, entrepreneurs and policymakers together in an unprecedented manner to fight the pandemic. This sparked the thought of capturing the megatrend of a new phase of industrial revolution, where collaboration between businesses, innovators and regulators would be a defining factor.

I am grateful to the HarperCollins India team for embracing the idea of *The Next New*. Diya Kar was generous with her guidance and advice. Sachin Sharma took up the project with a methodical plan. Shreya Lall was diligent and improved the chapters with her sharp editing. Special thanks to Kaveri Sengupta for her reliable research and sectoral briefs.

215

Mini Kapoor will remain on my list for triggering my journey as an author. Kanishka Gupta, as my literary agent, continues to be an enthusiastic supporter.

MarketsandMarkets has done stellar work by quantifying the megatrends changing the world. I am grateful to founders Sandeep Sugla and Aman Gupta for agreeing to contribute to this book. Krishnan Chatterjee championed the idea of the book from the minute I shared it with him. Aashish Mehra and the dedicated team of researchers provided several in-depth reports that added heft to the chapters.

I grateful for the blessings of my parents Saryu and S.R. Sharma. Sanchita and Aadi are the anchors of my life. Prashant and Sonia have always encouraged my work. They are bringing up their bright young children—Vasuman, Virochan and Anandini—in an increasingly digital world with careful curation of their screen time.

Many thanks to the band of boys—Manish, Rahul and Rohit—for their companionship.

# About the Author

Pranjal Sharma is an economic analyst and writes on technology, globalization and inclusive growth. He is an adviser to boards and international organizations.

A former head of Bloomberg TV in India, he has been a speaker at various fora in Europe, Asia and Africa. *The Next New* is his third book on technology-led transformations.

Pranjal is based in New Delhi. To know more about him, visit www.pranjalsharma.com

30 Years *of*

 HarperCollins *Publishers* India

At HarperCollins, we believe in telling the best stories and finding the widest possible readership for our books in every format possible. We started publishing 30 years ago; a great deal has changed since then, but what has remained constant is the passion with which our authors write their books, the love with which readers receive them, and the sheer joy and excitement that we as publishers feel in being a part of the publishing process.

Over the years, we've had the pleasure of publishing some of the finest writing from the subcontinent and around the world, and some of the biggest bestsellers in India's publishing history. Our books and authors have won a phenomenal range of awards, and we ourselves have been named Publisher of the Year the greatest number of times. But nothing has meant more to us than the fact that millions of people have read the books we published, and somewhere, a book of ours might have made a difference.

As we step into our fourth decade, we go back to that one word – a word which has been a driving force for us all these years.

Read.

Harper
Collins

HARPER
PERENNIAL

HARPER
BUSINESS

HARPER
BLACK

हार्पर
हिन्दी

HarperCollins
*Children'sBooks*

HARPER
DESIGN

HARPER
VANTAGE

Harper
Sport